TWENTY YEARS: AFTER "I DO"

TWENTY YEARS: AFTER "I DO"

Reflections on Love and Changes Through Aging

D.G. KAYE

Moyhill Publishing

Copyright © D.G. Kaye 2017

All rights reserved. No part of this publication may be copied, reproduced, or transmitted in any form electronically, mechanically, or by photocopying, recording, or otherwise, including through information storage and retrieval systems, without written permission from the author. Scanning, uploading, and electronic distribution of this book, or the facilitation of such, without the author's permission are prohibited. The only exception is the use of brief quotations in printed reviews.

Trade Paperback Release: November 2017
ISBN: 978-0-9947938-5-0 Paperback

Digitally Published: November 2017
ISBN: 978-0-9947938-6-7 Mobi
ISBN: 978-0-9947938-7-4 Epub

Contents

Dedication vii
Editorial ix
Also Written by D.G. Kaye xi
Introduction xiii

   Taking the Plunge and Commitment 1
   To the Moon with Laughter 7
   Unconditional Love in Sickness and Health 13
   Sex and Love 17
   Aging and Patience 25
   Sticking Around 33
   Sacrifice 37
   Traveling Adjustments 41
   Must I Repeat Myself? 47
   Remembering the Little Things 49
   When Retirement Approaches 53
   To Have or Have Not 63
   Earning My Wings 71
   Fighting Words 77
   Knowing 83
   Keeping on Top of Our Health 87
   Questioning Mortality 91
   Inevitability and the Will to Make a Will 95
   Epilogue 105

About the Author 111
Disclaimer 113
Acknowledgments 115
Other Books by D.G. Kaye 117
   P.S. I Forgive You 117
   Conflicted Hearts 120
   Words We Carry 121
   MenoWhat? A Memoir 122
   Have Bags, Will Travel 123

Dedication

I dedicate this book to my husband, the man who is grateful for my existence, keeps me grounded, supports my dreams, never denies nor falters, doesn't ask for much, keeps me laughing, and loves me to the moon.

Editorial

Twenty Years: After "I Do" shows not only newly married couples but also those in the middle of their lives how to navigate companionship challenges and show love and kindness to their partners, handling life together gracefully and in harmony.

Multibook self-help author D.G. Kaye demonstrates, using examples from her own marriage, how to really commit to a relationship—till death do us part.

Doris Heilmann, 111 Publishing

Also Written by D.G. Kaye

P.S. I Forgive You
A Broken Legacy

Conflicted Hearts
A Daughter's Quest for Solace from Emotional Guilt

Words We Carry
Essays of Obsession and Self-Esteem

MenoWhat? A Memoir
Memorable Moments of Menopause

Have Bags, Will Travel
Trips and Tales – Memoirs of an Over-packer

Introduction

As the years pass, our once wild and crazy times settle into the comfortable pattern of life, and only a strong foundation maintained through time can become the glue that sustains a fulfilling marriage.

Unforeseen circumstances will undoubtedly present a few obstacles. Illness can occur, potentially preventing us from performing certain tasks and prompting us to alter our lifestyles as we age. Plans can change unexpectedly, opportunities for travel may disappear, and even our interests can evolve with time. Despite putting forth our best efforts to remain healthy with good diet and exercise, we all have an expiration date, so it's our responsibility to maintain our quality of life by taking care of ourselves and nurturing our relationships with our partners so we may continue to enjoy and sustain our happiness.

My decision to marry a man two decades my senior gave me an education in learning to overcome and accept some of the obstacles and setbacks that can occur through aging. My husband's journey into seniordom presented a learning curve I had to adjust to before I could join him on that same path. Some of the blips along the way had me making decisions to circumvent newly arising issues. Sometimes, sacrificing some of my own plans or dreams was necessary so we could adapt to those challenges and continue enjoying our life in the manner we had grown accustomed to.

Our vows were tested several times through the years, and the promises we had made one another at the altar were challenged on several occasions, namely "Till death do us part" and "In sickness and health." But I took on each challenge as it arose, always seeking new methods to work around them—and despite those obstacles, keeping a relationship alive and thriving is possible as long as you build a solid foundation along the way.

When a house of love loses a few bricks while weathering some of the storms of life, only that cement foundation will keep the rest of the house from crumbling.

***Build that strong foundation,
because you'll need to rely on it
When the hurricanes of life blow your way.***

Taking the Plunge and Commitment

Before marrying someone two decades older than myself, I did my homework and weighed the pros and cons. I wasn't reckless, too young, or too naive to make that decision.

We met when I was thirty-seven and Gordon fifty-eight. I'd already lived through experiences beyond my years, and Gordon never looked nor acted anywhere near his age. Neither of us felt the gap between us. I searched my soul about committing to a man remarkably older than I was, because as one who was a frequent worrier about the future and the what-ifs, I needed to feel absolute certainty that my love for him would be enough to withstand whatever life could throw our way.

The ability to predict the future is a luxury we don't have. We can only remain optimistic, hoping the plans we make will come to fruition unhindered by obstructions. We don't expect, nor can we foresee, the possibility that our decisions may be countered by fate. But, with hope, we follow our hearts and go forth with what they desire, often without worry about possible unfavorable situations that may arise.

If I commit to something, I'm in it for life. "Till death do us part" is a simple phrase often not analyzed to its fullest extent as we bask in bliss, about to commit to our chosen life partner and join in holy matrimony. After all, who wants to think about possible frightening future scenarios on what's supposed to be one of the happiest days of our lives?

In that euphoric moment, while dreaming of a wonderful future together, we feel confident we can conquer any and everything. We feel invincible while shrouded with love as we stand before our friends and family, promising our beloved to love, honor, and cherish in sickness and health, often without taking in the truest depths of the words. We tend to discount the idea of sickness as a situation that will never happen to us—but often, it does.

Since moving away from home as a late teen, I'd had many suitors and a few marriage proposals through the years, but I had enjoyed my wings of freedom and had no desire to marry. Then I met Gordon, a man like no other I'd known. He was divorced and living it up, content to remain a bachelor. That was until he met me. On our third date, Gordon smiled at me, his sky-blue eyes twinkling with adoration as he embraced me in a warm cuddle, and announced that he was going to marry me one day. I had long resolved to never marry, but truth be told, I too by that third date had an uncanny feeling that I just might marry that man.

I laughed out loud, kissed his sweet cheek, and replied, "That will never happen." But it did. Our dating life left me more than enough material to write another book, but suffice to say, by the following year's end, we were living together, and within the following year, I was planning our wedding. I took the plunge after weighing all the fears I had about what the future might hold as older age set in against how much I loved and felt loved by this man. I couldn't deny the fact that I had found my soulmate.

After thirty-seven years of discounting any thoughts of marriage and never having experienced unconditional love as I did with Gordon, I realized that if I fled because of fears of the future, I may never find that kind of love again. After much internal deliberation and contemplation, I overlooked my fears about what might happen to Gordon in the coming years to end my bliss and decided it was better to have loved and lost than to never have loved at all.

When we got engaged, I was over the moon in love, but in one of my worrying moments, I turned to Gordon in a playful manner, demanding, "I want twenty years at least with you or no deal, mister." We both broke out into laughter. He pulled me into his strong arms and hugged me tight in that same manner that had always made me feel safe and protected, and he promised me twenty years.

This past October, we celebrated our eighteenth wedding anniversary, and December will mark our twenty-first year together from our first date. I have no regrets. We have a wonderful life together. We've built a strong foundation of trust, respect, laughter, and unconditional love. Those elements are the fundamentals that cemented our relationship, enabling our marriage to thrive through the good times and the blips.

Illness has found us both through the years and has taken a particular toll on Gordon. His stride and pace have slowed some, his posture is not as erect as it once was, and sometimes, in our silent moments in between conversations, I can feel his mind wander, deep in thought, before he turns to me with adoration and that familiar twinkling in his eyes and says, "We've been together twenty years."

I never ask him what provokes him to utter that statement, but I wonder if in those moments of silence, he reflects on my words of twenty years ago, demanding twenty years. I wonder if he's thinking about how fleeting those twenty years have been or if he's wondering to himself how many more we'll have together. But I don't ask.

I smile at him, nuzzle into him with a tender hug, and remind him how much we've been through together and how much I love him, assuring him we're buddies for life and beyond.

"Commitment" is a word we shouldn't take lightly. We commit to a plan even though plans sometimes change. We commit to go to the gym but sometimes fall short. We commit to love, honor, and cherish in marriage vows, yet some of those marriages don't make the long run.

Committing to a marriage is an ongoing job. The path through marriage isn't always paved with gold, and crossing some broken or tarnished steps along the way is natural. Life isn't always a neat bundle of perfection. On those days we feel challenged, questioning our resolve to stick around when unforeseen incidents place a wedge in our happiness, plans, or dreams, we must have all the essential components of a good marriage in place to withstand the cracks and maintain our commitment.

The decision we make to commit to marriage shouldn't become an afterthought. Sometimes, when clouded by grand illusions in our wedded bliss, we don't like to consider the possibility that we may have to swim through rough waters with the ebbs and flows of marriage. When our perfect lives are confronted with unpleasant issues, causing a bit of fraying at the edges and testing the strength of our relationships, we have to continue to mend those edges to keep them from unraveling into tattered threads.

When I decided to marry Gordon, I couldn't possibly have anticipated all the obstacles we'd face, but I knew in my heart that as long as I would love and receive love, we could face them together. I promised myself I'd be satisfied with however many good years of happiness I'd get with my husband, and that was enough for me, because that was more than the possibility of never having a second chance at grand love again.

I have no regrets in my stories, only truth and gained experience. My marriage has endured growth, circumstances, fears, and questions, and it remains a testament to love despite the tornados that have blown my way. Obstacles will always threaten to knock me down, and forces beyond my control will put my faith and commitment to the test, but when all facets of love are fulfilled and are enough to sustain the elements of marriage, age becomes a mere blip in the spectrum of challenges.

To the Moon with Laughter

A faded inscription etched into my wedding ring reads *Yuv You Cub*. Through the years, Gordon and I have come up with new words and different pronunciations for various words we invented in humor, ultimately leading to pet names for one another. It's been said one can judge how close two people are when they can finish each other's sentences or understand what the other is trying to say even if no one else does, sometimes even without speaking. I've mastered all those methods with Gordon.

Often, when we're joking around, Gordon will make up words to convey his meaning when he's unsure of a definition. I'll immediately understand what he's trying to say, and I'll chuckle with affection at his attempt and his desire to make me laugh. When we were dating, he never failed to remind me how much he loved me. He decided the word "yuv" had a stronger impact than "love," coinciding with his jovial personality, and he extended each declaration of his love for me by saying, "I yuv you to the moon," because he could imagine nowhere farther.

When we purchased our wedding rings, he had *Yuv You Cub* engraved inside the band so I'd always remember. Cub became his nickname for me not long after we began dating and remains the name he calls me by today. Gordon came up with the name after forming his first impression of me, or so he said, declaring that I was feisty, fierce, and as playful as a little bear cub. He laughed at his own sense of humor while informing me that Cub would be my new name. Gordon was just as fun, playful, and protective of me, and before long, I dubbed him a big playful puppy. And so Gordon became Puppy.

I love a play on words, creating a name from a shared quirky moment or inside joke resonating between me and a friend. Nobody else calls me Cub, but it wasn't long before my friends, who grew to adore Gordon, found the name Puppy fitting and so began calling him that too.

What would life be without laughter? I don't think I'd even want to know the answer to that question, because only with laughter have I been able to get through many of life's challenges. I could quote off a list of clichés about laughter, such as "Laughter is the best medicine"—but the fact is that it's true. Laughter is good medicine. Every good belly laugh allows our bodies to take in more oxygen and creates endorphins, which prompt the enjoyment we receive from humor and lift our entire wellbeing. Besides being a great health benefit to our souls, lungs, and state of mind, laughter can provide comic relief in those moments that sometimes aren't so humorous.

Based on all my relationships, I can attest to the fact that injecting humor in conversation when appropriate can take the edge off more serious circumstances. A healthy relationship will always contain humor, because laughter between two people creates a comfort bond, and comfort bonds maintain relationships through rockier times.

Although I don't profess to be a comedienne, I'm quite adept at bringing out the funny side of a situation when warranted. I can say with honesty that what first attracted me to my husband was his ability to make me laugh. Throughout my lifetime, I always felt I had to entertain and make others laugh, and until I met Gordon, I'd never been in a relationship with someone who could do the same for me. Gordon and I laughed a lot together as we got to know more about each other, and the pattern has remained a main ingredient throughout our life together. We found common ground on many things we valued and connected with, and I think the key was that we never lost our sense of humor no matter what each day brought.

I've witnessed many relationships head south when the initial attraction fades. Sure, people change opinions, preferences, or attitudes on certain issues as time passes, but if our core values or personality change, or if the common elements of enjoyment once shared between two people dissipate, we question our happiness. If we're not happy about our partner's personality change or views, a little bit of laughter dies within us. It becomes difficult to feel comfortable with our partner when inner unrest grows. The new discomfort curtails our ability to remain happy and feel the familiar freedom to laugh when our partner no longer shares the same humor. Note that I'm not referring to changes such as complacency or laziness that may set in due to declining energy levels. Age will sometimes alter our agility and even certain desires, but it doesn't have to affect our senses of humor. Age creeping into a good marriage shouldn't be a relationship killer.

I've been blessed. What woman wouldn't desire a husband who measures his love for her by the distance to the moon or to be reminded she's loved several times a day every day? Everything changes with time. The world advances at lightning speed. Our preferences change, our bodies change, our careers change. As the years pass, children grow and new family members are born, but the one constant in a firmly built relationship is undying love. If that love is deep rooted from inception and continues to grow, it can weather any of the elements of change the universe brings forth.

Laughter is a key ingredient to our wellbeing and keeps our spirits lifted. It's good for the soul and an essential part of the cement that bonds us through both the good times and the bad. If we can share humor with our partners in good times and in unideal situations, being able to overlook and laugh at some of our own shortcomings with humor instead of ridicule, we can look back with hindsight and see the comedy after experiencing our not-so-humorous moments.

The ability to make little private jokes with a partner that only we can understand is a personal sharing that can go a long way in keeping a relationship vibrant and fresh. It also keeps the doors to our hearts open.

Unconditional Love in Sickness and Health

Unconditional love was an unfamiliar term to me, unrecognized for most of my life because I'd never experienced nor believed it existed. My understanding of unconditional love was that it meant loving a person no matter his or her faults or beliefs. I thought it meant partners love us regardless—warts and all.

Through sickness, devastation, defeat, and blame, if somebody loves you unconditionally, he or she will stick around and still love, support, and compliment your attributes even when you're at your worst.

Before I met Gordon, I'd never experienced such love. Old scars of shame and low self-esteem have had the propensity to linger within my psyche. As an ordinary, awkward-looking child, often overweight through my childhood, I'd had my share of being ridiculed. Even through the years of trying to fix myself and learning to grow my self-esteem, those haunting memories of my long-ago past of feeling inadequate still occasionally circulated in my mind.

I often obsessed about how fat I looked or how a partner could still desire me if he saw me with no makeup on, once all my naked flaws behind the glamor were exposed. The insecurities I harbored when I was younger were engraved in my memory because I had nobody lifting me up, encouraging me to feel worthy about who I was on the inside. Some of my relationships had also kept me discouraged, as men couldn't resist reminding me I may have gained a few pounds.

But when a man can see you in your most dire moments of humiliating illness and isn't the least concerned about a few pounds, when he's able to look at your bare face in the morning and hug you dearly while telling you how beautiful you are with sincerity in his heart, he's a keeper. Gordon is that man. Many relationships aren't strong enough to weather the storms, but illness is a good indicator of the strength of a relationship.

When the bad times came barging into our relationship after we'd been married for only one week, Gordon was there for me. He stood by me, not only out of a sense of duty. He cleaned up my sick messes, fed me when I had not one ounce of strength to lift a spoon, and complimented me even when the steroids I was taking to save my life made my face and body round and distorted. He cried with me, told me countless times a day how much he loved me, and reminded me that to him I'd always be beautiful, that we'd do whatever it took to make me better, because he didn't want to live without me. That was when I learned about unconditional love. That was the lightbulb realization after our vows kicked in early: I had chosen the right man to share my life with.

Since that first illness tested our bond, we've both faced several more health issues and gotten through them together. For Gordon, my health issues became the gift that kept on giving. Then it was my turn to reciprocate when he was diagnosed with stage IV prostate cancer eight years ago. Gratefully, his life was spared, although he experienced every single side effect imaginable from the radiation, which he still endures on a daily basis and rarely complains about. And when he gets a little down in the dumps about his suffering, I remind him how lucky he is to be alive and to have the privilege just to complain. He smiles at my reminder and counts his blessings.

With the remnants of Gordon's cancer treatment, and after almost losing him again in 2016 to liver disease, we spend a lot of time at the doctor's. He has treatments to keep him healthy as can be, and I'm determined to do everything I can to keep him functioning so we can maintain a joyful and active life. It's an ongoing project, orchestrating doctors' appointments and treatments between our work schedules (yes, he's still working!), filling out forms, and keeping track of his medications, his diet, and even his bowel movements because of frequent bleeding episodes courtesy of the radiation proctitis (medically induced colitis) he lives with, but we manage.

Many of my new responsibilities are in relation to my husband's aging process and his body not tolerating reactions to the illnesses he's acquired through the years. But whatever the reasons, it's my turn to give back my unconditional love. I'm a long-time believer in "Where there's a will, there's a way." If there's a better way to help my husband, I'm always searching, and I'll find it. Unconditional love means loving someone no matter what comes. Unconditional love is not about an obligation to do the right thing, not about standing by and doing what needs to be done. It's about doing things out of the goodness of our hearts, loving without limits.

Sex and Love

A strong foundation, mutual love, and respect are the recipe for a healthy sex life. Although I'm not about to exploit our sex life, I will say maintaining a healthy sex life within a marriage is important. The physical exchange between two people in a loving relationship is a demonstration of desire. As every new relationship grows, sex plays a major part in the early lustful stages when chemistry ignites desire, which is part of the attraction.

But dating sex will eventually turn into married sex. Spontaneity may not be as frequent, and the duration may lessen depending on the time we have. We hear it all the time, people complaining that sex in their marriage has diminished as the years pass. Yes, life happens. We get busy, children's needs take precedence, circumstances arise, and often sex becomes the thing that suffers in a relationship, falling to the bottom of the list. The bed becomes something we can't wait to get into just to go to sleep. But in a healthy relationship, quality can replace quantity. In keeping the sparks of passion alive, everything else has to run smooth—communication, respect, and compassion.

Aside from the lack of time, it's easy to understand why sex disappears in many marriages. If one partner becomes distant, self-absorbed, or uninterested in the other's life, you can bet resentments will build within, and eventually an invisible barrier will form between both parties, creating an emotional distance. Some people may notice the dwindling attention, but some may not even realize so much time has passed since their partners last complimented them, asked how their day went, or even bothered to offer a kind gesture to show their appreciation or affection. Couples often get used to living in a declining pattern of communication and recognition, leaving themselves asking, "What happened to us?"

Life blazes along, and with no awareness, we can get caught up in a lifestyle we fall into instead of choosing. Even in the best of relationships, sex can subside because of time factors and interruptions and because, through the passing years, love often replaces lust. That's where building that strong foundation early in a relationship will play an important role. However, when lust turns to love and then love fades too, there isn't much left to hold the bricks together. If we've already lost respect, consideration, and attention, there's no incentive to evoke or ignite desire, sometimes leading us to question whether we even want to remain in that relationship. But sometimes, despite everything between two people running smoothly, illness strikes, hampering what's left of a sex life. This can become a test of the strength of the relationship, when a seemingly healthy shared sex life becomes threatened by illness.

Ten years into our marriage, Gordon and I still enjoyed a healthy sex life. We always made time for sex, and it remained a spontaneous act, which kept the sparks ignited. For Gordon and me, afternoons were our favorite time to make love. In the morning, we were always eager to hop out of bed to tackle the day, and at night, we were often too tired, or Gordon went to bed before me. So we named our little escapes "afternoon delight"—until one day, things were no longer delightful. Oh, sure, the passion and desire remained, but a certain part of Gordon had somehow lost its will to join in the party.

This pattern continued for about a week. Despite Gordon not being able to perform, I had no insecurities about our relationship. I didn't wallow in a sea of "I'm not good enough" or "I don't turn you on anymore." Instead, I suspected a problem, and after suggesting he try that little blue pill a few times with no results, I made him a doctor's appointment. Up to that point, Gordon had been having his PSA levels tested as part of his annual physical to check for prostate cancer. I'm an avid researcher of medical issues, but until Gordon's new issues developed, I'd never had a reason to research that disease. We hadn't been made aware from his past results that there was anything to be concerned about, but when I went with Gordon to the appointment and found out his count was substantially higher than I would have found acceptable, and without getting into disputes and semantics, I requested that he see a urologist.

A few weeks later, Gordon and I sat in the small stark waiting room at the urologist's office. It was our second visit awaiting the results from the tests and the painful biopsy he'd endured. By that time, I'd been doing research on the many possibilities that could have been cause for Gordon's symptoms, and I'd focused my deductions on a diagnosis. He had an enlarged prostate, which is common in men over the age of sixty. Anxiety held a firm grip on my emotions while we waited our turn to see the doctor, but I was hopeful.

Several magazines rested on a table beside my chair. Although I flipped through a few to pass the time and attempt to divert my overwhelming worry, I wasn't paying any attention to what I was reading.

The doctor called out from his office doorway and invited us in. He took a moment to acknowledge us by raising his head, interrupting his reading of the file he had pulled from a manila folder. Our eyes made contact, and the doctor nodded as if to say hello before we took a seat. My calming force within was taking comfort in the fact that we had one of the best urologists in town, despite his age and his nearing retirement. His eyes projected a quiet demeanor and kindness.

We'd sat down for only a moment before he read out the results from the file and took a slight pause for a moment before announcing that Gordon had stage IV prostate cancer.

In that moment, I felt as though my body had shut down and frozen. I took another moment to register those frightful words that pierced my heart as the doctor continued sharing detailed findings and presented us with a plan of action. Gordon sat motionless, taking in every word the doctor spoke. I burst into a sea of tears. I couldn't control the well of emotion that filled me as though I'd just been sucker-punched in the solar plexus. My brave husband, without a single tear in his eyes, reached over to hug me, reassuring me he would be okay. He was consoling me.

The doctor offered comforting words along with his plan of action, detailing what would ensue. He explained that to complement the upcoming radiation, he was optimistic that administering testosterone-suppressing injections would halt the growth of the cancer, giving me back a thread of hope that Gordon might just beat it. By the time we left to go home, I had left behind the horrifying moment when I felt my heart fall to the ground and had my mini breakdown. There was no way I would allow my thoughts to linger around the dark side or for one moment allow myself to even think about a life without my husband. From that day on, Gordon and I worked on a plan to get through the journey together. Never once did we mention any what-ifs or any negativity.

I'd arranged for us to see our naturopath, Dr. Eric, to begin Vitamin C intravenous therapy within a few days after receiving the evil edict, because radiation wasn't to begin for a few weeks. Vitamin C in mega doses can't be tolerated orally but is a well-known therapy to attack cancer cells. There was no way in hell I was giving those damned cancer cells the liberty to grow and multiply before we could blast them with radiation.

After thirty-nine rounds of radiation treatments and three years of biannual hormone-suppressant injections into his groin with a foot-long needle to deter the growth of new cancer cells, Gordon Junior was pretty much dead. The oncologist informed us that after the treatments were all finished, within a year or two, his PSA would most likely rise to a normal number of two or three again, which would have been a maximum acceptable limit for his age, as testosterone would once again circulate. He also said Gordon would regain his sex drive.

It has now been seven years since Gordon's treatment. We visit the oncologist twice a year to ensure his PSA levels are in check, with no flags. Testosterone levels remain at zero, as production never resumed. Gordon was a trooper through it all. The radiation, injections, and Vitamin C therapy he endured had produced a miracle. Gordon was pronounced, and remains, cancer free.

So what happens when the sex goes? Life continues with lots of love, hugs and laughter, and a whole lot of gratitude. My fears of potentially losing my husband and my worries about his health as the radiation aged and slowed him down didn't leave me much time to complain about my new nonexistent sex life. That was not a concern at the forefront of my mind. Taking care of my husband was, and there were plenty of other things to do together that became more important than sex. Gordon's illness only made the bond between us stronger. My determination to make him well again, and Gordon's overwhelming adoration for me for standing by him and taking care of him, never faltered.

Illness can be a tricky thing for some relationships, becoming a marker of their depth and strength. Because of our foundation built on love and commitment, our relationship had endured an important element we lost, an essential component of a relationship: sex. But this didn't destroy everything else we had. We could still hug and cuddle and make each other laugh. Our commitments to each other withstood the test of illness. The cancer didn't kill him, and it didn't kill us.

Ironically, during Gordon's treatments, as though God had chosen that specific time in my life, came a new development. I began experiencing severe symptoms of menopause. With the new women's issues I was enduring, the last thing on my mind was sex. Divine timing? I'm not sure, but call it what you may, the universe has a funny way of making things happen at the right time.

Gordon was the perfect patient. He never complained once throughout his treatment and has since encountered a host of unpleasant residual effects from the radiation. He has occasional flare ups of radiation-induced colitis because of the maximum radiation pointed at his prostate, which damaged part of his bowel. Although on occasion he may blurt out he's sick and tired of the damaging effects when his colon acts up, I remind him that the worst is over and the side effects are a small price to pay for having his life back. He'll concur and smile with his little-boy charm as he's reminded he's lived to fight another day, and the grass is greener on this side.

Aging and Patience

Time can potentially rob us of our abilities and often slow down some of our motor skills. As Gordon ages, I notice the subtle changes that sneak up on him. The hands of time seem to push their way into our lives, affecting some of the habits we often take for granted.

I nicknamed my husband the man on a mission shortly after we began dating. His inner wheels are always spinning. He's always one step ahead of himself, always doing two things at the same time. No matter the activity, he's quietly thinking about something else he must attend to. These thoughts will include work, his to-do list, and even matters I look after for him as his personal life secretary—scheduling all his appointments, plans, medications, trips, and bills.

I am grateful for his remarkable memory, which is often better than my own. He'll remind me about a phone call I forgot to make, an appointment I forgot to change, or an item I forgot to add to the grocery list. He's great with remembering dates and birthdays and has an uncanny memory for numbers, and his addiction to watching sports keeps his mind active, storing statistics, scores, and injuries of all the players in both hockey and baseball. His obsession with never being late for anything also makes me wonder whether he ever really sleeps deeply. I'm convinced he has an alarm clock in his brain that awakens him ten to twenty minutes sooner than necessary.

When Gordon gets an idea in his head, his impulsive nature spurs him to act on it at once. It took me years of trying to get him to slow down, reminding him to enjoy the now, to stop worrying about the next thing without enjoying the present. I realize his ongoing desire to focus on the next task goes hand in hand with his fast-paced thinking.

Before his body took a beating from cancer and liver disease, Gordon was mighty and speedy. His broad chest and muscular arms and legs supported his love for physical work. Throughout our many moves, he has built us beautiful backyards, decks, and sheds, laid sod, planted trees, and mowed our lawns. The two of us took on the task of renovating our last home by ourselves, only having to sub out the plumbing, flooring, and electrical work. His precise and talented carpentry skills, which he learned in his much younger years when he helped build homes for his brother, came in handy for us as homeowners. When we owned our own homes, he kept himself busy when he wasn't at work, and he thrived on it. I could always find him in the backyard or garage, fixing something or watering the grass (his favorite pastime) or the plants in our gardens (sometimes near to death).

With Gordon, more is more. More is always better. If something is on sale, he wants to stock up. Everything becomes stockpiled. In fact, our storage rooms are nicknamed Costco. Even after having sold our last home and downsizing, becoming renters, I struggle to keep him from wanting to stockpile when we shop.

I was convinced, because my man on a mission was always on the next thought or project, his quick-paced stride was part of his speedy package. I can't begin to count how many times I've scolded him over the years because of his ongoing habit of walking several paces ahead of me no matter where we were going. Many things have changed through the years, but Gordon's aging became most evident to me when I realized I'd become the one who walked well ahead of him. No longer do I have to hasten to keep up. I now find myself having to stop every few feet when we're walking together, allowing him to catch up with me. Gratefully, he still walks on his own two legs without any required aids, but his natural spry gait has mellowed now from a race to a stroll.

Sometimes I'll reflect on the moments I used to shout out to him, "Wait up! Where's the fire?" I now chuckle at and long to have back those very times when I felt that frustration of being left behind, and my new frustration at these changes sometimes gets the better of me. My husband, who had always walked five paces ahead of me as though he were in some dire hurry to get wherever we were going, ironically now walks a few paces behind—an uncanny reversal of order.

Missed turns when driving are another issue. I shout, "Turn here" several times before approaching the street, giving him fair warning but sometimes going unheard, and we often miss the turn. Once again, I'll sigh and mumble that either he doesn't listen, or perhaps it's time to get his hearing checked, which often leads to a nonsensical argument. And once again, I'll feel remorse for my outburst.

I know he's doing his best. I know his hearing isn't as sharp as it once was. I'm not angry at him. I'm frustrated that time has robbed him of his once staunch alertness and reflexes. I must keep reminding myself that my age hasn't progressed as far as his yet, so we aren't aging at the same pace. I get to watch him grow old. When I notice the changes and reflect on our history together as lovers and chums who did everything without hesitation or obstacles, I want to go back there. I want the clock to go back, but it can't—and these are the thoughts that pass through my mind in my moments of frustration.

Gordon's slower pace became something I had to get used to, but it's still a hard bite to swallow. Sometimes I just want to shout, *Move, I'll do it!* or *I'll fix it! I'll lift it!* when he's attempting to do something I know I'm going to have to finish myself anyway, but I don't. It's not his fault that it takes him an extra few moments to complete a task that was once second nature to him. It's not his fault when I'm waiting for him to catch up to me, even if I stand tapping my foot, muttering "Hurry up" under my breath. I know he's doing his best, and I'm so proud of him for still accomplishing all he does. I know my frustration is really about my not wanting to accept that he's getting older.

Agility is just one of the many gifts of life that we so often take for granted. As we age, our bodies don't always keep pace with our minds. Often relationships entail some role reversal. The once cared-for become the caregivers, and the love tested over with time becomes the cement that carries us through whatever comes next. In my moments of melancholia, I remember our earlier years together, the years where I depended on him so much. I have no problem now stepping up to the plate and taking over for some of the things he used to do. It just makes me sad sometimes.

I think about how Gordon must feel to have had to become reliant on me for some of the more mundane household chores he used to do without thought. The simple act of climbing up a stepladder to change a lightbulb is my job now. Oh, yes, he'll still fight me on it, telling me it's no big deal to climb up, but it is. The last thing I want to see is my husband, with his unsteady balance, on a ladder. Instead, now we do lightbulb changing together. I'll climb up the ladder and ask him to hold me steady while I unscrew burnt-out bulbs and hand them to him. In turn, he'll hand me a new bulb. When I get off the ladder, I hug him and tell him it's still teamwork with us, just in reversed roles, and we laugh.

Loving and caring for a partner who is advancing in age is a true test of commitment to a relationship. Long after the wild good times have rolled, the dust settles into the true essence of love. The party shoes become slippers, and the two of us have become like the matching sweaters we've worn to weather the many obstacles we've faced together. Through the years, we've applauded one another's successes, taken turns looking after one another, dedicated our attentions and priorities to one another, and built those bonds essential to forming a foundation for love and respect.

The fact that Gordon's aging came to fruition before mine was the reality I chose not to focus on when I married him. I wasn't ignorant about the inevitable, knowing that nature would undeniably take its course. I just chose not to dwell on it and live life every day in gratitude for my happiness. To be honest, I couldn't even picture ourselves as older, but aging isn't something that suddenly happens. It's a process. It's a string of days in a well-lived life that turn into months and then into years. The daily living of events tallies up, and the afflictions of life, health, and genetics result in the sum of how we function in our senior years.

We may not always feel age coming on, or we may choose to ignore the signs of slowing down, creaky bones, duller reflexes, and loss of strength as aging sneaks in, creeping up on us silently like a thief in the night, but eventually life will call it to our attention, and once the signs have announced themselves, we begin looking for the workarounds—the fixes and cures, the bandages for the ravages of time to help keep us functioning, to keep the music playing in a relationship. At least that's how it feels to me.

But despite all the changes, we're still happy, and I'm grateful to still have my wonderful husband in my life. Aging can rob us of many things, but it can't diminish true love, and it doesn't stop us from laughing. In fact, if you can joke about some of the obstacles of aging instead of wallowing in what has changed, you can still celebrate many good things. Laughter is part of our daily interaction. It was what drew me to my husband when we first met, and it's a part of what's cemented our life together. If there's laughter, there's love.

Sticking Around

Some days are harder than others.
I look back at the golden days when love was fresh and exciting, the days when I didn't worry about the what-ifs of tomorrow because today was robust with vigor and verve. Our social calendar was brimming with plans, and our dreams for the future were something to look forward to. We were busy living and doing, and I didn't worry about the possibility of time slowing down or hampering our enjoyment of life. Through the passing years, our love and respect for each other have grown deep enough to sustain some of the changes time has brought forth into our lives, especially with our health issues.

We enjoyed entertaining and hosting dinner parties, going out for dinner and dancing with friends, before a new comfortable sense of complacency set in, quieting some of our activities as the years passed. We grew comfortable in our own surroundings, and although we still enjoy the company of our friends and loved ones, the dancing days began to wane.

Gratefully, Gordon loves to work. He thrives on the challenge of keeping up with or breaking his own car sales records. Myself, I worked my entire adult life, and when Gordon requested I stop working when we got married, I didn't protest. I had to adapt to a new routine to fill my days. I'd never been the type to sit around and watch TV, but the thought of becoming a housewife was appealing to me because it was new and different.

For the first few years of our marriage, I woke with Gordon at dawn's first light to fix him breakfast, pack him a healthy lunch, and kiss him goodbye before he left for work. I ironed his shirts, searched out new recipes, and cooked dinner each night. I enjoyed doing all these things for him. With time, I no longer woke up at dawn to make him breakfast, although I still packed his lunches and made us dinner.

It was during the early days of my new stay-at-home life that I began studying health and natural remedies. My obsession with becoming proactive about our health stemmed from the onset of my near-fatal diagnosis of Crohn's disease, which struck me within the first week of our marriage. My determination to help heal myself as well as keep my husband healthy became a priority.

My studies kept me busy, and my voracious appetite for reading and researching had me itching to write about what I was learning. I began submitting articles to health magazines on my findings about Crohn's disease and journaling about my adventures, life lessons, and experiences having grown up with a narcissistic mother. I fell into a rhythm of self-satisfaction and felt content with our life together as it progressed.

As a lifetime social butterfly, I had wings that would have been impossible to clip, and one of the main reasons my marriage worked was because my husband never put a leash on me or tried to dissuade me from my aspirations. He understood my inner mechanics soon after we met, and he loved me for all that I was, with no intentions or expectations of changing me or my elusive desires, always cheering me on with every new idea I wished to pursue.

Gordon is a clever man. He always knew how to handle me. He's supportive and complimentary and tells me every day how much he loves me, and I in return do the same. All these factors are part of the cement that has been poured into the foundation we've built to sustain our marriage. It's nothing for Gordon to walk into the room and ask me, "Have I told you today how much I love you?" His crystal blue eyes light up from within every time he reminds me.

I'm fortunate. Many couples have slacked over time with these little gestures of love because they figure they may have said those words of endearment enough, or it's taken for granted and understood that each partner knows he or she is loved. But not expressing our feelings or reminding one another that we are loved and valued has a propensity to create some distance between a couple. Everybody wants to feel validation in some fashion from a spouse, and it's amazing how small gestures of affection can recharge our happiness batteries.

With that said, we are always growing, and many of our interests do change through the years. This is where acceptance comes into play, because neither of us has ever tried to change the other. We take the time to listen to what each other has to say without dismissing any of our thoughts as trivial. I'll listen to Gordon's sports talk because I know he desires to share his enthusiasm or disappointment when his favorite team wins or loses, and I'll talk about my writing accolades and pitfalls even though he may not grasp the essence of my stories. He doesn't hesitate to cheer me on or pick me up when I'm feeling discouraged. Communication lines are kept open between us, and this is part of what bonds us together.

Times change, health issues come up, desires are born and lost. The dancing shoes begin to collect dust, but the music plays on when we tune in to other channels. Sometimes people flee when the going gets a little rocky. Commitments to remain united get broken plenty of times, but what lies in those commitments is what will become the difference between fleeing and staying. When two people are each other's rocks and have stored up a lot of goodness in their relationship, doing things willingly for one another without having to be asked, that goodness becomes the building blocks of a solid foundation. When trouble strikes or the good times cease to roll and life tests us, nobody is running away, because no resentments or hurts have cracked the cement in the foundation.

Sacrifice

When I chose to marry Gordon, I didn't live in a fantasy world, unconcerned about the future. I didn't jump in recklessly, thinking life wouldn't present problems down the road. I wasn't delusional, thinking, *I'll worry about whatever happens when it happens* or *Nothing bad is ever going to happen to him*. No, I took everything into consideration and thought logically about marrying Gordon, and knew in my heart that the bottom line was that I loved him for all he was and who he was and that love, providing it was reciprocated, would sustain me through whatever came our way.

⁓ ⁓

When I talk about the sacrifices we make in life, I'm referring to sacrifices we make for our marriages, our children, or sometimes just for the sake of peace. But what are we sacrificing? Do we become heroes because we act selflessly by giving into or giving up something to someone, by sacrificing our own happiness for others? Do we sacrifice to appease, or do we sacrifice from the goodness of our hearts?

"Sacrifice" isn't a simple word. Sacrifice in a marriage isn't an accolade we should brag about but an act we perform voluntarily for the pure pleasure of giving up something we desire for the sake of someone else's happiness or need. A healthy relationship involves a give and take from both parties, and if one of those parties isn't reciprocating, he or she isn't sacrificing. When we commit to an honest relationship, we realize that selflessness is a main ingredient and part of what strengthens the bond as our relationships develop. We accept that life consists of peaks and valleys, and we sometimes have to give up something with an open heart to accommodate our partners' needs.

If we're the selfish type who only take from a relationship what we want and flee when obstacles present themselves, there is no sacrifice, only selfishness. Sacrifice will always be part of a good and healthy relationship because that's what we do when we love with our whole hearts: We give of ourselves with no complaints or expectations.

So where does the word "sacrifice" fit into my relationship? Am I supposed to say I sacrificed my midlife years because my husband is older now and we're unable to do many of the same things we once did together in our earlier years? That's not how a good marriage works. I didn't sacrifice anything to be with Gordon. We've had a wonderful life together and still do. Sure, our age difference can sometimes present challenges, but what marriage doesn't encounter challenges? Ours are just different. We care about each other and have always been at each other's sides through the big moments and the small. We support each other's desires, dreams, and ambitions. We make each other laugh and remember to tell one another "I love you" every day. Our views on certain issues will differ, and sometimes Gordon may not understand my writing life, but he's proud of me and applauds my accomplishments—and he never complains.

If I'm lost in my work and the dinner hour has passed, he won't complain but will help himself to a bowl of cereal. My husband is a good sport when it comes to my desires, and he's always happy to see me happy. That's how it's been since the beginning of us, and that says a lot for why we're still together today.

A good relationship always entails sacrifices. Maintaining a good relationship is like creating a recipe with all the nutritional ingredients and flavor, well simmered to ensure it's tasteful and fulfilling, and part of that recipe is to be generous with hugs. Hugs are a loving expression of our emotions. Still, to this day, when Gordon makes me laugh with his boyish charm, I see the charisma that attracted me to him twenty years ago and can't resist hugging him like I would a comforting teddy bear. He is my teddy bear, huggable, lovable, dependable, helpful, and caring. So really, what could I possibly have sacrificed to receive all the gifts I am given?

Traveling Adjustments

Travel is my passion.

Wait! Let me rephrase that: Having arrived at my destination is my passion. The actual act of traveling is no longer a pleasurable experience for Gordon or me, and traveling with a senior involves a little more planning.

I enjoy going to new places and revisiting old favorites. Escaping to warm, sunny destinations from the drudges of our Canadian winters is my favorite of all vacations. I may not always be able to take off on a whim as I used to do a few years ago for a girl getaway, but Gordon and I still love to travel.

We both enjoy the sun, ocean, mountains, and meeting new people, but getting to those places can sometimes prove a hassle with all the regulations at airports and with the airlines. Too much luggage has always been an issue with me, and it seems the older we get, the more items we pack to have on hand in case we're unable to obtain them in certain locales. Packing our medications and foods requires preparation and a lengthy what-not-to-forget list. Our trips are not the spontaneous ones we used to take when we were able to jaunt off on a whim, but we still enjoy getting away when we can.

When I was single and traveled, I always managed to be offered a helping hand with my numerous bags from kind strangers. It sometimes paid off to look like a damsel in distress when I struggled to lift bags off the carousel or into the overhead compartment on an airplane. When I got married, my husband took over the task of schlepping and lifting bags. As much as he'd complain about my too many bags, his chivalry was relentless when it came to the heavy lifting, but it's not like that anymore.

Baggage control is no longer just an airport rule but one my husband tries to enforce on me. Whenever I'm packing for an upcoming trip, he'll remind me that he's no longer able to lift or retrieve, and the onus is on me. Gone are the days when he'd stand on duty by the carousel, awaiting our bags, often missing a round or two before he'd effortlessly grab each one off the belt. He'd often release a snorty grunt and an eye-roll directed at me to signal his disapproval for my having to take advantage of the full fifty-pound allowable weight per bag. But nonetheless, he did his husbandly duty.

I've now become the schlepper of all bags, the lifter of bags off the carousel, and the one who struggles to lift our overstuffed carry-ons up into the overhead cabin bins. Since I've inherited this task, going to the gym two to three times a week has come in handy. When one spouse can no longer pull his or her weight, the other steps up. This is how we roll, and I do so without complaint—or maybe just a few grunts. But carrying, lifting, and pulling bags isn't all that has changed. There's a lot more pre-planning involved when traveling with a senior, especially when having to remember to pack all the essential items to maintain our health while away.

Purchasing travel insurance is crucial, as is reading the fine print. As our ages go up in number and pre-existing illnesses recur, I've had to be diligent in making sure my husband is covered in case any potential illness strikes while abroad and to ensure we don't go broke from health costs if something were to happen. Travel insurance is an additional financial expense that must be included in the cost when budgeting for a vacation.

In our earlier years together, Gordon's work plan covered such costs, but now we must purchase this added insurance prior to every trip, since his work's plan stopped extra coverage at age seventy. Once we've booked a vacation and before purchasing the travel insurance, I re-read the fine print and call the insurance carrier to double-check the coverage and make sure any changes to my husband's condition and medication are covered. Countless times, I've seen people on the news who've been denied coverage when they needed it on vacation because of the various gray areas in many policies. The coverage must be black and white to ensure peace of mind. It's a tedious procedure, but essential.

We all know that the airlines charge extra now for just about everything … except the recycled air we breathe. They squish in as much seating as they possibly can get away with for more revenue, and aside from paying for a seat—though it's beyond me why the seat isn't included in the price of the ticket—there's a higher premium for rows with extra leg room. Thankfully, I'm still in half decent shape, still able to contort my body to adapt to the cramped quarters of a plane, but Gordon now pays the price of being squashed in like sardines, with terrible leg cramps that set in only hours after we've landed and persist for a few days into our vacation.

We've also taken to wearing masks on the plane because of some of the illnesses we've returned home with after flying alongside coughers and sneezers, caught in the mosh pit of microbes. Once upon a time, we were fearless, unafraid of germs, throwing caution to the wind. We took our chances we wouldn't catch a cold or a flu. It was a fifty-fifty gamble, and the worst we'd caught was a cold until 2016, when we both caught influenza on a return flight from Phoenix, Arizona. There happened to be a large outbreak in the state while we wintered there, and while we managed to dodge it at the time, on an airplane home with over two hundred and fifty passengers and continuous coughers, our number was up.

When a senior has health issues and the immune system becomes compromised, he or she is more susceptible to contracting illnesses. That bout of influenza knocked me for a loop and had me out of commission for more than a week, but it almost cost Gordon his life. Wearing a mask on the plane has since become an essential part of our travel regime.

Something else I've taken to doing on recent trips is putting Gordon in a wheelchair at the airport. Although he's perfectly capable of walking, the long journey through airports sometimes proves too much for him. Having him in the wheelchair helps save him from walking to the gates, which, by some phenomenon, wherever we may be traveling to, always happen to be the farthest ones. The same applies to our return trips, where the walk to customs after deplaning can be a good mile in distance.

Using a wheelchair also allows us to check through the priority lines, saving Gordon from having to stand for a lengthy wait as well as from having to bend down to remove his shoes and then put them back on. It also allows him to pre-board a flight, which is helpful in giving me space and time to lift those carry-ons into the overhead bin without pushy people already blocking the aisles and creating chaos, holding up passengers from getting to their seats. It also keeps me from worrying I'll drop a bag on someone's head—something that has occasionally happened!

Must I Repeat Myself?

"Dinner is ready!" I holler from the kitchen to my husband, who is addictively tuned in to a sports game on TV in his man cave. When I summon him from a mere thirty feet while setting the dinner table, there's no reply. Again, I'll shout his name at a louder decibel, usually to no avail, until the third time, when I dial up the volume, almost screaming to be heard. He'll then stroll into the kitchen after hearing me or by instinct at the waft of food or the echoing clang of pots and pans as I prepare to serve dinner.

On other occasions, I may walk into his man cave to ask him a question and note that his eyes are glued to the TV and he hasn't noticed my entrance until I stand right in front of him. He'll then look at me with questioning eyes, wondering what I came in there for. I'll ask him, and his usual response is "What? I can't hear you." I'll repeat my question over the blaring of the TV, and then he'll respond with his usual reply: "You don't have to scream. I can hear you."

But I do have to scream, because he doesn't hear me when I speak at regular volume. "We need to get you a hearing aid," I often retort.

Gordon will reply, "I don't need a hearing aid. I can hear you just fine."

That isn't so, of course, but I continue to let the issue slide no matter how many times a week we go through the same scenario.

Many nights while I'm working on the computer in the living room, Gordon is watching TV in the room behind me. On the other side of the wall I sit against is the TV in his man cave, but I'm the type of person who can't concentrate with noise while I work. The volume of his TV reverberates behind me like a nagging echo, often sending me into a tizzy. It's become a standing routine that I go to his room and request that he turn down the TV. I'll have to listen to his same defensive whining about how he can barely hear the TV once he's turned it down, yet he remains adamant that he can hear just fine.

Ironically, not one conversation between us has transpired in the last year or so when Gordon hasn't had to ask me to repeat what I've just said. The situation is like a catch-22, because he'll first tell me he can't hear me, and no sooner will I repeat myself in a louder voice then he'll respond by telling me, "You don't have to scream. I can hear you." I then remind him I do have to scream because he didn't hear the first time. It becomes a worn-out old song between us, leaving me wondering whether there's a happy medium I can find somewhere between talking and shouting. I'm still working on it.

Remembering the Little Things

Gordon prides himself on his great memory, and I can attest to it. His long-term memory is sharp and intact, and often his short-term memory is much better than mine is. He's always been astute about keeping on top of appointments and all other responsibilities, but sometimes it's the little things I've always taken for granted about him that he now sometimes misses.

I've always been a paranoid person when it comes to locking doors—house doors and car doors. I trained Gordon well since the beginning of our relationship with my obsession about making sure to lock the door as soon as we leave or re-enter our home, and he always abided by my quirks. But once in a while I'll find myself walking past the front door after he's returned from work and notice he's forgotten to lock it. I'll bring it to his attention in a joking manner, and in true Gordon style, he'll come up with an excuse as to why he didn't lock it automatically: "I had to run to the bathroom" or "My hands were full when I walked in. I was going to lock it after I put things away." He'll use a handful of other excuses for variety, but the fact is he never used to forget or postpone. We step inside and we lock the door. It used to be second nature.

My husband is no chef by any means, but I sometimes allow him to fry up an egg or warm up a bowl of soup on the stove. I know he's never grown accustomed to the digital era with several appliances, and this has become a concern for me, especially if I'm not home to double check that he has turned the stove off.

Gordon has always been fiercely independent, a quality I've admired about him. I don't enjoy sounding like a nag, as much as I know I have tendencies to do so, but I feel it's necessary to keep an extra eye on things. I'm sometimes even concerned if I find he's been in the bathroom too long. I'll call out to him to make sure he's okay. These are just some of the instinctive actions I've grown to take after the many health issues he's encountered, especially since I almost lost him last year after he passed out in the bathroom. These incidents have instilled an inner alarm system within me, alerting me to pay attention to all his activities.

I'm a professional worrier. Every time he goes to work, I ask my angels to watch over him while driving. I've become a backseat driver when we go out together, as while Gordon is a good driver, there are many on the road who aren't. I have an uncanny ability to predict when a car is going to pull a wonky move on the road. I'll warn Gordon ahead of time when I feel the car in front is going to cut into our lane. I'll instruct him to wait for the light to turn red before completing his left-hand turn because our roads have become lawless, with incompetent drivers speeding through red lights. I worry for him when he's out driving on his own, praying he'll come home safe.

My concerns came along with time. When you know your spouse and know what he or she has been through, all his or her weaknesses and shortcomings, you worry. Nowadays, when my husband isn't home, there is no such thing as out of sight, out of mind. Growing older with a partner who is well into his golden years brings forth concerns about everyday things I may not have given a second thought to when we were younger. In a sense, it's almost like babysitting. And when it's your baby, young or old, you want to look out for him.

Do I drive my husband crazy? Without a doubt, I can say I know I can be overbearing, but sometimes when I'm behaving too much like a mother hen, Gordon will remind me that he's not a child. I may respond in jest by telling him he is a child, my child. But after several minutes pass, he'll come to me and hug me with one of his cuddly bear hugs, thanking me for taking such good care of him.

When Retirement Approaches

My husband has worked hard all his life. He grew up on a farm, helping his parents maintain it. The farm was to become his legacy until the day his father was unfortunately killed by a passing train. In the exact moment his truck crossed the tracks, the train sped by. Gordon was only fourteen years old. Back in those times, train signal warnings weren't automated. The person in charge of manning the signals was on break, and there were no flashing lights or whistles to warn drivers. Gordon's family farm was eventually auctioned off so his mother could afford to look after her eleven young children.

At twenty, Gordon decided he would move to the big city, Toronto, and focus his efforts into selling cars. As it turned out, he rose to become one of the top salesmen in the city, selling cars for General Motors, and remained so throughout his forty-eight years at the dealership. There's no financial security as a commissioned salesman, no pensions, and if you don't sell, you don't get paid. But Gordon has done well for himself. He built a wonderful life and supported his family well.

In 1999, we also made ourselves a good life together. Because he was already approaching sixty, I suggested we hire a financial advisor to help us plan for his future retirement. But no matter how well one plans for the future, there'll always be setbacks, because investments rely on expected profits for the coming years, and markets fluctuate and sometimes tank in the global economy.

Back in 2000, we thought by the time Gordon was sixty-five, we wouldn't have a care in the world, but through the years, some shaky real estate times, and when investments got hit, we restructured our finances. We had smart planning, so the economic crash wasn't as devastating to us as it became for others, but that coupled with the rising cost of everything had us thinking sixty-five might not be the magic number he would retire at.

Fast forward to 2010: Gordon was approaching his late sixties and still working. He was in his forty-eighth year at the same dealership when the owner's younger family generation restructured the company. Consequently, remaining top salesman was no longer relevant, because younger blood was thought to increase sales. Management requested Gordon retire. As a parting gift in recognition for his years of service, they gave him a brand new Cadillac, a tidy sum of money, and a retirement party. The whole event came on without much warning, and despite the gifts of recognition, Gordon was unhappy and shocked at the restructuring.

This turn of events had us reassessing our financial plans and forced me to digest the fact that my husband would now be home all the time. As much as I love my husband, I had grown to love my independent time while he went to work. I began to worry about what he would do to fill his days and keep himself busy when all he'd ever known was the dealership. What would Gordon do? I worried about him staying engaged mentally and physically, wanting to keep his brain occupied and his butt off the couch all day.

Gordon worked many hours a week, and, as expected, he'd built up quite a large clientele through the decades. He was well respected in the industry and by multiple generations of customers. Gordon's gift of an uncanny memory allows him to remember the make and model of every car he's sold. I know my husband thrives on the interaction involved in making a deal, and I was concerned about him no longer working at a job that had fulfilled him for most of his life. There aren't many left in the industry of his ilk. He's still an old-school type of man who always goes the extra mile to satisfy his customers. If there's a problem after sale, he never fluffs them off to the service department. He'll arrange for the customer and car to be properly looked after, somewhat a lost art in today's world.

After Gordon was asked to retire, I worried about his sense of worth, whether he'd become bored at home with no mental challenges or social interaction to keep him engaged. I knew we had a solid marriage and enjoyed each other's company, but his going to work kept him happy and kept me looking forward to the end of each day, when he'd return home. I was concerned about us being home together day and night.

About a week had passed since Gordon retired. Word had spread throughout the many dealerships who knew him well, and his phone rang several times a day with friends in the business calling to inquire about his sudden departure and customers looking for him. Many calls came from owners and managers of other dealerships, friends he'd worked with and for through the years, hoping to entice him to come work for them by offering him lucrative perks. They all knew his work ethic, and they knew how profitable it would be to have Gordon come work for them, but Gordon needed time to digest all that had transpired. His ego was bruised, and he was still far from accepting or understanding why he had been asked to retire after dedicating forty-eight years of quality service to a dealership with a top-notch sales record. He wasn't yet ready to make any decisions.

In the meantime, Gordon had taken to watching TV day and night in his man cave, and despite the many daily interruptions from him in my own new way of life, I was concerned about his state of mind. We had several chats about possible new avenues he could explore, from taking up one of the many offers to work at another dealership to possibly working from home on the wholesale end of selling cars. Gordon was offered many managerial positions, which he declined, as he always had done through the years at the dealership, claiming he could make more money on the floor with commissions than on a fixed salary. He always said he didn't need the headaches or the long hours of being a manager.

And so, a few more weeks, eventually turning into months, ensued during which I watched my husband become a shadow of his former motivated self, and I wasn't happy about it. Finally, after several phone calls from a long-time friend Gordon had worked with throughout the years, nagging him to come work for him, dangling several carrots and offering Gordon the opportunity to work on his own schedule, Gordon came out of retirement and went back to work at age seventy-three. His decision to go back was not only a boon to our finances, but it calmed my stress levels. I was relieved that he once again had a purpose to wake up in the morning.

Retiring involves myriad decisions and emotions. We often dream of the day we'll retire without considering what happens after the glow of newfound freedom wears off. Men and women are wired differently when it comes to the daily grind. Most men don't realize what it takes to micromanage all the everyday things the wife does in a household. They aren't always aware about what goes on behind the scenes to keep a home running on a daily basis and how much of our time is spent shopping, cleaning, and doing errands. If a man doesn't have any hobbies other than watching sports on TV incessantly with no job to go to, or has no chores to tend to, it's easy for him to become complacent, overweight, unhealthy, and depressed with no stimulation to keep the brain challenged and engaged.

Depression was where I worried my husband might have been headed. Of course, the same symptoms can apply to women, but most women have outlets. They have friends and family to share their concerns with, a support system. They have hobbies and chores that fill empty hours better than most men do. Men don't tend to want to share their innermost thoughts with others, sometimes harboring depression. I've heard about many men throughout the years who retired and withered away, some even dying not long after retirement. I wasn't about to let my husband become one of those statistics. We all need an agenda and goals to keep us motivated. Motivation fuels the body and mind. Too much time on our hands can allow us to dwell on worries, which become stress factors.

In 2014, the housing market had been reaching ridiculous values. Although these exorbitant new prices kept rising in the Greater Toronto Area, we lived in a northern suburb of the city where prices had escalated but demand hadn't quite reached its full capacity. People were becoming worried that the housing bubble was on the verge of bursting. Gordon was now halfway into his seventy-sixth year and becoming concerned about what would happen if he retired and the housing market were to crash before we sold.

We'd been contemplating selling our home because Gordon no longer wanted to climb the stairs to get to the bedroom, and the cold Canadian winters were taking their toll on him. He decided we should sell our home while we'd make a small profit, invest the money, and rent a condo where the interest on our investment would cover our living expenses and enable us to go away for a few months in the winter. If we remained in the house, we wouldn't be able to maintain it while disappearing for a few months.

As much as I felt the market was still escalating and urged Gordon to wait one more year before we sold, it was a gamble. He was nervous the bubble was on the brink of bursting and feared if it did, we'd be stuck in the house for enough years for the market to turn back around, and that would mean no winter escapes until we sold. His concerns caused me internal panic, and as much as I felt it wasn't yet time to sell, I worried that if he was right, and if we waited until it was too late, he wouldn't get to fulfill his wish of winter escapes after working all his life. So we went over our plans and finances with our financial advisor and decided to take the plunge. We were comfortable in the fact that we could go forth with our plans.

Our house sold in two days. We made a small profit from the house we had lived in for only two years after buying and gutting it to make it beautiful. I thought we'd get a lot more than we did for our house, but we accepted the deal and moved. That first year after, houses went up another twenty-three percent, and the stock markets took a bit of a beating. Needless to say, my stomach churned with the thought of how much we had lost in the hit and how much more we would have gotten for our house had we waited just one more year. The sum of both those actions would have left us in a much more profitable position, but I never wanted to be the "I told you so" person, so I lived with my lumps. Now, two years later, the price of housing in our city is still outrageous. New families can't even afford a starter home, and the government is only now trying to come up with new restrictions to contain the unheard-of prices, which have spread far beyond the city limits.

Selling my home at the wrong time still stings when I think about its current value, but I can't dwell on the what-ifs, and I'm always grateful for tender mercies. When the universe works in its magical ways, it reminds me that life has a way of working itself out. One year after we moved, my husband took very ill for much of the year. Subsequently, he was unable to work, spending many visits in and out of hospital, almost at death's door twice. While I took care of him and worried plenty, I thought about how grateful I was that I didn't have to worry about the upkeep of a house. As it turned out, God was good, and by August of 2016, Gordon was well again—and yes, he went back to work!

Of course, Gordon can't keep working forever. Gratefully, his employers are so good to him. They appreciate his service and grant him the freedom to work the days and hours he chooses. They understand what he's been through and that some days he doesn't come in because he's not feeling up to par, or because of the many doctors' appointments he needs to go to. But his desk awaits him even when he takes off for two months for a winter escape.

In many aspects, despite selling our home prematurely in a still escalating housing market and leaving some money on the table, things have worked out for the better. The peace of mind factor is by far the best part of the decision we made. Another great benefit of living back in the city is that we are in close proximity to all of our doctors and the hospital. It used to be a long drive to everywhere, especially to doctors.

Being married to a senior often frightens me when I worry about the future. I don't like to dwell on or even allow myself to think about dark scenarios, but as a realist, I sometimes drift into concerning thoughts about when my husband's time on earth will come to an end and I will be left without him. I know now when that time comes, I at least won't have to worry about carrying a house, or having to endure the sale of it while in the desperate hours of grieving. Once again, I'm reminded to count my blessings for the mysterious way the universe seems to work.

Retirement is a simple dream, a time in life where our work is done and we can relax and enjoy the golden years. When making decisions about retiring, it's important to consider how we'll fill in our new leisure time and keep ourselves active as well as planning financially for the future. It's not uncommon for us to say that we'll retire at age x, but life circumstances can prolong retirement or bring it sooner than expected, potentially derailing plans.

Financial crises can become a reason to delay retirement no matter how well planned, just as an onset of a debilitating illness can provoke an earlier unplanned retirement. Because we never know what lies ahead, it's important to plan well and be prepared for inevitable mishaps. I'm sure glad we had a plan, even though it got altered a few times.

To Have or Have Not

I have no natural children of my own. My decision about whether to have children has weighed heavy on me since my early twenties. I was too busy celebrating my newfound freedom after moving away from home at eighteen and putting my self-esteem back together, beginning to enjoy life. Getting married and having children was the furthest thing from my want list. While I marched down many an aisle as a bridesmaid for friends and relatives' weddings, those events left no residual desire panging within me to follow suit. Sure, thoughts of the future crossed my mind plenty, but I couldn't envision myself having children.

I questioned myself often through the passing years, wondering whether my biological clock would tick away and I'd later have regrets. As the years passed, as much as I thought I didn't want children, I still wondered whether this was selfish of me. I wondered whether I was enjoying my freedom too much or perhaps might change my mind if I found the perfect man. Maybe we'd both want to create a new life between us.

But after my many moments of contemplation, I'd go back to living in the present, once again dismissing my thoughts of having kids. During those moments,

I'd sometimes project my thoughts to the future, to my golden years, and find myself in a panic with more what-ifs. What if I grew old and had no children by my side to take care of me when I needed looking after? Those thoughts scared the crap out of me yet had me questioning my scruples and motives. Did I really want to bear some fruit from my loins just because I worried about who would look after me in old age? Was I being honest with myself on my reasoning for not wanting to have children?

I was young, in my twenties, when the question became like a nagging thorn hidden in the back of my mind. Did I want to procreate? Although I had plenty of friends who'd already begun families, looking at their little ones' cute and burbling smiling faces never jabbed at my maternal instinct, causing me to pine for one of my own. Don't get me wrong: I love babies, always have, but I just didn't have the same longing within that many girls my age had had since they were little. I was never that girl who daydreamed about meeting her prince charming and raising a family. I was fine with my decision, save for the odd moments those little nagging thorns would rear their prickly heads, having me seeking reassurance for my decision, which had yet to seem final.

I thought a lot about why I had no interest in raising a family, and the only reason I could come up with was that I'd already done it. I'd been there and had the T-shirt. My dysfunctional childhood with a mostly absent mother had left me looking after my siblings since I was young. I was the eldest, so I had shouldered the responsibility. I harbored a lot of resentment toward my mother while I was growing up. I had babysat for my siblings since I was twelve. Even before then, I had been cooking, doing laundry, and carrying out several other designated chores while my mother indulged in her life of leisure. I dared not complain to her, for my delicate ego couldn't tolerate her lashing out at me with fits of screaming and domination, letting me know she was the mother and I didn't get to question what she said. Instead, it was just easier to do what I was told.

Despite my household duties, my most peaceful moments were when she wasn't home, which was often, so it became somewhat of a fair trade. I would do everything a mom is supposed to do as long as she wasn't home to disturb my peace. It's a sad truth, I know, and my childhood gave me plenty to write about, but it also left scars and an overwhelming feeling that I'd had enough of taking care of children and didn't want to have to do it all over again. My upbringing played an enormous part in my procrastination, eventually leading to me not having any children. But that isn't to say that my worrisome little thorns didn't continue to pop up from time to time as my mid-thirties approached.

Those were unhappy years for me, as I found myself trapped in an abusive relationship, where the last thing I needed was to become pregnant. My focus then was primarily seeking a way out, which left little time for those nagging thorns to even be given any consideration. But, by the grace of God, I broke free after fighting dearly for my release. Swallowed up by a host of life lessons, I took my emotionally battered self and put her back together—and in the midst of finding and celebrating my newfound freedom, I met my future husband.

I was content, happy as a sleeping child to be on my own for the rest of my life, when I met Gordon. He'd already been married, had raised a family, and had been resolved to remain a swinging bachelor until he met me. A mystical chemistry was ignited between us on our first date, a chemistry I had only ever known once before in my younger life, and although it was exciting, it frightened me when my intuition signaled that my single life was about to come to an end.

Throughout our relationship and before we were married, those pesky little thorns pushed their way up to the forefront of my brain, reminding me that this was the last train ride to motherhood, forcing me to decide whether I wanted to hop on. Not only did I have to confront my resident thorns, I had to envision myself doing most of the raising of a child if Gordon and I were to create one. Flowery thoughts of having a little Gordon or a mini-me had me imagining many scenarios about our possible little bundle of joy, but the realistic visions demonstrated Mommy taking care of everything, running to little league or ballet class, going through the teenage turmoil when I'd be in my fifties and Gordon well into his seventies. An even scarier thought was the possibility of becoming a single parent if something were to ever happen to Gordon while our child was still young. There were many conflicting visions on my part, because I knew Gordon well enough to know that the last thing he wanted was to become a father again at almost sixty years old.

We discussed the possibility of having children numerous times, mostly because I was torn with indecision. I knew Gordon loved me to death and would move heaven and earth to make me happy, even if it meant giving me a child, so ultimately, the decision fell upon my shoulders. He as much as told me that he'd do whatever made me happy, understanding that I'd never had a child. He told me that he would most certainly love and provide for our child but in the same breath admitted that I'd be doing most of the raising—whatever Mommy says.

I battled those lingering thorns back and forth from subconscious to the forefront as we planned for our wedding. Only days after, I became gravely ill. Within the first five months of our marriage, I went in and out of the hospital a few times, was put on terrible, debilitating medications, and endured many tests before I was diagnosed with Crohn's disease. There wasn't a lot of information available on that disease back in 1999, nor were there any effective medications but several rounds of steroids to halt the inflammation, leaving my immune system with a whole new host of side effects to combat as well as the disease.

With the first two years of my marriage spent being sick, the drugs began eating away at my muscles, hindering me from walking without the occasional stumble. I was still taking birth control pills at the time, and my doctors advised me to get off them, because they weren't good for my condition and the other medication I was taking. Amidst all the craziness, I couldn't even begin to deal with reminders from my thorns. I had to make a final decision about having children at a point in my life where I wasn't even sure I was going to recover or live long enough to raise a child. Gordon was sick with worry that he'd almost lost the love of his life, so the thought of having children was the least of his concerns. Inasmuch as this was the case, he was petrified about the what-ifs. What if I were to become pregnant after being taken off the pill? So he came to me one day while I was lying in my sick bed and informed me he was going to have a vasectomy. I was in no mindset to contemplate the finality of his decision, and to be honest, my mind felt at ease because Gordon had made the decision for me. There would be no babies.

I'd wrestled with my thorns for almost two decades at that point, and somehow at that pivotal moment in my life, I let go of all the burden to make a firm decision about having children and passed it over to my husband.

The following years, I was busy working on regaining my health. I did a lot of research on my disease, surfed the web on the new computer Gordon bought me, and began my journey into healing. Within a few years, I'd gotten off all the drugs, gotten my sense of self and my body back into shape, and began seeing a naturopath and taking supplements to calm the flareups that came with my disease. And I moved on with our life together.

Do I have regrets about not having children? I never paid much thought again to those old prickly thorns. I was healing, and I no longer had that heavy decision weighing me down, a decision I could never seem to have come to terms with previously. I resolved myself to enjoy and be grateful for getting my life back with a man who supported and loved me every step of the way. Sure, there are moments when both Gordon and I talk about the what-ifs. He'll laugh, joking at times, saying if we had a little Cub, she would be a little high-maintenance girl who'd go get her nails done with Mommy, or a little Gordon who'd most likely be double the handful for me that Gordon already is. We both chuckle at what might have been, but in the end, we are just grateful that we have each other.

Earning My Wings

It's often said age is just a number. I follow that camp of thinking. Age was just a number when I was younger and dating men who somehow always seemed to be older than me by at least a decade. Sure, people can label my relationships with many old clichés—father figure, security-status seeker, or whatever the flavor of the month is—but I never looked at them in that manner. Rather, I knew I'd jumped from childhood to adulthood early in life.

At a young age, I was looking after my younger siblings and pacifying my father's wounded soul. I seemed to relate more to adults than I did kids my age. Dating older men never left me feeling as though there was any age gap between us, because we had much in common, so age difference was never a factor in my dating decisions. But when I realized the seriousness my relationship with Gordon was taking on, I did have a few worries about our gap. As our relationship grew, it wasn't the number that was an issue but my growing realization of the future and my projected concerns. What might lie ahead for us with our age difference? When we're younger, we don't often worry about the future, but when we step into those future-predicting shoes, we find ourselves thinking about potential concerns that lie ahead.

I'd already been through all the decision making, though, and the bottom line for me was that love trumps all concerns. I decided that when age showed its true colors, I'd have already been in the relationship long enough to grow with it, and I'd be willing to take on whatever would come our way. Shit happens, and so does aging. Nobody standing outside a marriage can judge what transpires between two people. Sure, people can make assumptions. They can question the age gap of a relationship and form their own opinions, as people often stereotype couples with notable differences between them.

There is no harsher critic on a relationship than the concerned daughter of a father marrying a younger woman. I can speak from experience, because my father was divorced, and because of his meek and sometimes naive demeanor, he attracted many of the "wrong types" of women. A daughter can sometimes be overprotective of her father. I wished for years that my father would heal from the wounds my mother had engraved on his heart and hoped he'd meet someone who'd appreciate his worth. I wish he'd found someone who'd have loved him and taken care of him. Unfortunately, that never happened, but he at least had my sister and me.

Through the years, my father dated some shady women, women who didn't appreciate him for what and who he was but rather went out with him to see how much they could extract from him. It boiled my blood when I'd ask him about what was happening in his life, hoping one day he'd tell me he'd met someone nice, but instead he'd tell me about yet another woman he'd dated, what she'd demanded of him, and what he'd given her. It hurt my heart that my father never met a woman who could appreciate him and all his goodness and that he never received the love and care he deserved. Like most daughters, I guarded my father fiercely, the same way a lioness hovers over her cubs. I'm not one to jump to conclusions, but after years of experience since childhood, I'm astute at assessing relationship issues. My interest in observing people and their behaviors grew with me through the years.

But not everybody wishes the same things for their parents. Some children, young or adult, can't fathom the thought of their parent being with anyone other than their other parent, often disregarding their parents' happiness. Some children will never accept the new partner as worthy enough, refusing to feel anyone is the right color, background, or age. That is where ripples in the waters form between that parent and child, and the parent's new partner has to learn to walk a fine line as he or she comes closer to being a permanent fixture in the parent's life. Dancing around the emotions of children from a previous marriage can prove to be a challenge.

I know about such challenges, as I've been on both ends of the spectrum. In my younger life, I was my father's protector. When my husband and I first married, he had four grown daughters who were all not far apart in age from me. I was concerned about how or whether they'd accept me—and asking for acceptance isn't something we have a right to do. Rather, we must earn acceptance.

As a new wife, I couldn't just place myself in my husband's family and expect everyone to welcome me with open arms just because their dad loved me. I had to pass through stages before my husband's children would accept me as their father's new wife. I'm not referring to being accepted as a stepmother but to being accepted as good enough to fill their requirements and be welcomed. Not that being accepted is a prerequisite for all new wives entering a second marriage with a previously married man, but it can make family life a whole lot easier.

I knew from my experience with my own father that Gordon's family would be observing me before I were to, if ever, be accepted by them. I understood that and respected that. My own scrutinizing over my father's relationships had me gauging the worthiness of the women in his life. I made it my business never to interfere with things that had to do with Gordon's decisions as a father, but I also never felt I had to explain or validate my relationship with him, nor to plead my reasons. I only had to be myself and let life with us take its course. Those around us who'd spent time with us and kept abreast of our life together had only to learn through what they saw how good I was for Gordon, despite whether they liked me or not.

Living life and going through circumstances together reveals our character. Time is the great teller, and our true colors show up when circumstances arise through the judgment period. Once I'd proven my unfaltering love in the scrutinizing eyes of Gordon's children, after they'd witnessed the affection, respect, and happiness we exuded, the ice thawed, and, organically, I became part of a family.

Fighting Words

I was teased a lot as a child, sometimes by the kids in school and sometimes by my own family. I lived through it and learned to grow a thicker skin, to build my self-esteem and overcome my childhood inadequacies. After spending a lifetime listening to my mother belittling others, I witnessed and felt the humiliation of those upon whom she inflicted her cutting words, my father in particular. I learned at a young age just how powerful words are, often cutting much deeper than a physical wound that heals faster.

Because of the verbal abuse I witnessed and the impact it left on me, I learned how painful words stay with us and how they can leave a scar after slicing the heart right out of a relationship. Even in the best of marriages, there will be disagreements and bigger arguments. This is human nature, as we all sometimes stand on different sides of certain issues. That's what makes us all unique—our standards, values, and morals. Though a marriage may be solid and strong, there are days when anger falls upon us for whatever the reason. It's how we handle those moments of discord that sets the tone for respect. If we cross boundaries using angry words that take us beyond the issue at hand, that leaves residual damage to the relationship well after the original issue of contention is rectified.

Controlling our emotions in difficult times while we're feeling hurt or angry at a loved one is a delicate balance. In those dangerous and sometimes thoughtless moments when we wish to shoot off our mouths or bang the door closed, it can be a challenge to hold our tongues. While seeing red, we may not always be able to see the repercussions if we allow ourselves to unleash our words of anger.

Fair fighting can sometimes feel difficult to maintain. When we find ourselves wanting to expel our anger, it's essential to pay attention to the manner in which we direct our words and discontent. We want to defend our cause and have our protests heard in that moment of heightened discord, but we also need to consider how others will interpret our words in those moments to avoid tainting the future of the relationship. It's doable, but it's a fine balancing act. Expressing anger without turning the argument into a personal attack is a delicate art, as is keeping the discussion contained to the context of the original conflict.

I don't profess to be an expert on anger management issues, but my experience growing up in volatile surroundings has served me well in learning how to deal with situations of the heated variety. I admit, I'm blessed to have a wonderful relationship with my husband, but that doesn't mean we don't have our occasional disagreements. Throughout our relationship, though, no matter the arguments we may have had, neither of us has ever lashed out with mean or derogatory words. I call this fair fighting. Every relationship is different, but I consider my methods of dealing with the occasional unpleasant incident worthy because they're effective in making a point while cooling the fires of the immediate moment.

I like to use the "count to ten" theory: Before I respond to an injustice, I count to ten and take a pause to think about how I'll voice my opinion to avoid saying something hurtful. I find this effective, not allowing my mouth to react before my brain takes a few seconds to assess what comes out of it. My aim isn't to punish someone with hurtful words but to discuss my displeasure with the issue at hand. Once we spew a hurtful word, that word will remain in the receiver's memory long after apologies and forgiveness take place. It's easy to say we take back our words, but they become a stain in the archives of our minds.

If an issue arises that upsets me and I've tried to make my husband aware of my discontent, but he perhaps hasn't yet digested my point and leaves the room in a huff, I'll refrain from further conversation. I've learned long ago that there's not much point dragging on an argument after I've shared my side. There's no need to escalate emotions while he's in defensive mode. I'll plead my case and walk away. This gives us both time to settle down with our emotions and mull over the issue at hand.

We may think men don't listen and just move on from an argument as though nothing has computed, giving us the impression they don't give a shit, but they do. They often just have their own methods of processing what's transpired in their own time and manner. By keeping an argument clean, without accusations and name calling, allowing time for logical assessment, we're quashing the flames, preventing them from turning into a wildfire. My silent timeout gives us both a chance to cool down and reflect. It sometimes may take a whole day and has sometimes taken two days before Gordon and I digest a problem and are ready to re-confront one another with an apology. Neither of us is too proud to apologize, and both of us aren't happy when we're not speaking.

It's also important that I know my husband understands the reason for my displeasure, because an apology without realizing what he's apologizing for, just for the sake of apologizing, doesn't rectify the initial problem. If I'm the one who feels wronged or slighted and has called for the silence between us, I've developed a pattern through the years where I'll walk away. When I do, I'll tell him I'm not his friend right now. After a few hours of giving him the silent treatment, he'll approach me with his devilish grin, attempt to hug me, and ask if I'll be his friend again. He'll cajole me and pose the age-old question, "Don't you love me?"

And I'll reply with my usual response, "I love you, but I don't like you right now." It's important to note the distinction between the words "like" and "love." Arguing with my husband doesn't discount the love I have for him, only expresses my dislike of the situation. He'll mope around until he's ready to put his pride aside and apologize or until my guilt surmounts and I approach him with small talk to break the ice. That's his signal from me that his punishment is over and we can discuss why we had the disagreement with calm and level heads.

He'll make his usual comment in those situations: "Oh, you're talking to me?" But as much as he'll try to sound surprised or smug, I know he's relieved. It's important to note that just because I may have taken a timeout from speaking to him, I'll never be vindictive. I'll never resort to hurtful tactics. Just because I'm not talking to him doesn't mean I won't cook him dinner. My silent treatment isn't a vengeful retaliation, rather a timeout to reflect.

I'm content with my methods of resolution because they give us both time to process the conflicting issue without fanning the flames. We don't throw personal insults into the mix, which can bring long-term repercussions far beyond the original argument. Many couples who allow their arguments to escalate into harmful rows harbor emotional hurts from unresolved issues from the past. Those issues surface from time to time once a new disagreement arises. That's why it's essential to address and rectify each issue as it comes rather than allowing resentments from the past to accumulate and resurface in each consequent situation. If old hurts aren't rectified, they remain dormant and manifest in future arguments. What we don't let go of festers within.

Knowing

In his quietest moments, I can hear him thinking. He's always thinking. There's no silence in Gordon's head. Even while watching TV, his mind is busy spinning. His thoughts may be focused on anything from the customer who's coming in tomorrow to an item he's remembered to remind me to pick up at the grocery store—or, often, he's thinking about me, some old memory he'll feel compelled to remind me about.

Often when speaking to him, I'll notice his concentration focused on something other than me. He'll claim he's listening to what I'm saying, but his attention is on something else within. I call it attention-span lapsing, not quite ADD but more like brewing an idea while in the midst of a separate conversation. These little moments used to drive me crazy in the early stages of our relationship because I felt as though he wasn't paying attention to our conversation, but he was. He always did. I hadn't yet learned how his mind worked.

I've had plenty of years to study my husband and can read his thoughts just by a certain look on his face, a silence between us, or sometimes from the first word of a sentence when he speaks. Even the manner in which he'll call out my name prompts me to know what he'll ask me. When he calls me Cubby with a higher pitch and an emphasis on the *y* sound, I know he's in a jovial mood and eager to share good news or something funny. When he calls me Cub, I know he's going to ask me a question or has something pressing on his mind he wants to share. Deb is reserved for his pissed-off moments.

We've always been so in tune with each other, spoken words or not. Many times, I'll walk into his man cave, and he'll be watching TV, not even noticing I'm there as he focuses with eyes glued on whatever he's watching. I'll announce myself after standing to his left with one of my usual smart-ass comments, "Earth calling," and he'll turn after I startle him, chuckling because he knows the thought police is on to him.

Based on whatever may be currently going on in our lives, I have a reasonable idea about what he may be dwelling on in his moments of silence. I'll remind him he's home now and it's time to turn off his brain and relax. He'll smile with that familiar twinkle in his blue eyes and once again ask how I always seem to know what he's thinking. I don't know how I know. I just do. After spending so much time together, we grow an inherent understanding of the silent language interpreted by eye contact, a lack of it, body language, silence, temperament, or sometimes even by the bang or the silent closing of a door.

The thought police in me is always on duty, ready to dissect Gordon's brain. It's become second nature.

In this past year since Gordon's health suffered, I have noticed how much more he likes to remind me about some of our best times we've shared. Sometimes I know he's trying to get a rise out of me with laughter. Other times I can't help but feel he's thinking about his mortality. I don't dwell on it, nor do I let him know I know what he's thinking about.

Nobody ever wants to think about the end of existence. But trust me, as we age, we all have many of those days when we feel the hands of time ticking by. Gordon's brushes with death have somehow opened the curtains of a window he never previously cared to look out of, a window he never talked about—one we've never talked about. But I know that window revealed to him how close the end almost came for him in the past year, causing him many pauses for thought. He doesn't say so, but I know.

Once in a while, when Gordon breaks a silent moment between us and says in mere passing, "We've been together twenty years," I know where his brain goes. I never ask him to elaborate on where those thoughts come from, but I know when he's in a reflective mood, when he feels the urge to relive tender moments, when he's fearing his mortality. In those exact moments, I know.

Keeping on Top of Our Health

If the years have taught me anything, it has been to become more conscious of how precious life is. I used to think I was invincible when I was younger, that nasty diseases would never happen to me. I learned fast that train of thought was a complete misguided perception. The reality is that our health deteriorates as we age, and parts of us may not function as they once did in our younger years.

When I dared to look back at the passage of time and digested the reality that my parents and their parents had no track record of living out healthy and long lives, it frightened me. Both my parents died of coronary issues. My father died at age fifty-five of a massive heart attack after already having suffered a few others and a stroke at age thirty-six. My mother suffered years with heart issues since her mid-fifties, surviving many more years than her doctors expected, before she finally succumbed to her ill health at age seventy-four. Her parents died before nature's clock should have allowed, also of terrible diseases.

These alarming statistics burrowed themselves in the crevices of my mind as I got older. No longer did I think I was invincible. The rude awakening prompted me to become proactive with my health to help prolong my longevity. When I was diagnosed with Crohn's disease and close to the brink of death, I knew I had to take my health into my own hands and became proactive about getting myself well. My research had me questioning my doctor's medical approaches, leading me to change my family physician after allowing my illness to continue until it got dire.

In my research, I studied many drugs and their effects while enduring the debilitating side effects of the medications I was taking. I searched the Physicians of Ontario website to find a reputable naturopath, and I did my homework well. Dr. Eric and I formed an instant friendship. I made note of his credentials and learned about his studies and the amazing research he'd done in Germany, which he brought to his practice. He now hosts one of the most advanced complementary medicine and cancer clinics in Toronto.

Dr. Eric and I had many interesting conversations through the years, and without a doubt, he's given both me and Gordon quality of life back many times over. He referred me to a new physician who works in conjunction with naturopathic doctors and is willing to prescribe homeopathics before pharmaceuticals. I've also learned to keep copies of our lab tests to share with my naturopath for his opinion and assessment and to enable him to direct us on whether we should take certain prescriptions or an alternative after receiving a Western doctor's diagnosis.

I have also made a conscious effort to choose doctors closer to my age or younger who keep up with medical advances. Forming good rapports with all our doctors enables me to ask informative questions, and making a list of questions to ask them before going to an appointment helps so I don't forget. After several encounters with doctors and specialists, I've learned that by being friendly and knowledgeable about our medical conditions, I gain their respect, and they're more eager to offer those extra few precious moments of their time. Also, forging good relations with the secretaries helps if I have a special request or question I need help with. If I find myself concerned with a symptom or drug effect, I'll phone my local pharmacist, because a pharmacist knows more about drug interactions than a doctor does.

Both Gordon and I take natural supplements prescribed by Dr. Eric to keep our engines running at their possible best. We try to live healthy and make the best of what we have by staying on top of any new issues that arise and keeping up with all doctors' appointments, never putting them off and hoping symptoms will just disappear. All these efforts are part of taking proactive measures to maintain good health as we age. I've made it a priority to put together a good medical support system. I can say with certainty that between all the health setbacks Gordon and I have endured, staying on top of medical issues has helped us gain favor with doctors in desperate times.

When emergency strikes, we're not always in a stable frame of mind to remember things such as all the medications we take, what types of vaccinations we've had and when, or every symptom or allergy we've encountered. It's important to keep copies of our prior lab work, notes on vaccinations, and a list of current medications in a personal file for easy reference. I also keep names and phone numbers of all our doctors handy in my mobile phone. We are all entitled to a copy of any tests we've had done, so I make a point to always ask for a copy from our doctors. I'm only too familiar with illness on different fronts, and I'm grateful for the many times I've had those files handy and up to date with our medical history.

As the years accumulate, it seems, so has the number of doctors' visits. When I was young, I had an aversion to doctors. But as I age, I look at going to a doctor's appointment as a gift. Taking care of each health issue as it arrives in a timely fashion has added to our quality of life many times over.

Questioning Mortality

I was in my mid-forties when a close girlfriend of mine lost her battle with cancer. Her death hit so close to home with me and signaled my first realization of my own mortality. She was a single mother to two young teens when she passed. She had a personality bigger than life and had never been sick before, but she was no longer once the beast, cancer, snatched her away. That was my first reckoning with just how suddenly the grim reaper could pull a fast one on us.

It's funny how when we're younger, we're so focused on living for the moment, and thoughts of old age or mortality don't niggle in our minds. But as we age, such thoughts have a propensity to visit with a little more frequency. Losing a close friend in my early forties was my first real wakeup call to how short life really is, and it sure drummed up a little more anxiety about the prospect of death. It's the culmination of experiences we encounter—illness, financial setbacks, and burying friends and loved ones—that helps to initiate a new awareness of what lies ahead.

When we're forced to confront unpleasant issues and re-examine painful events we've endured, we grow and mature. The reality and finality of life has a way of creeping into our subconscious. When I was a young teen, I'd already witnessed my father taking ill and had lost my maternal grandfather. In my early twenties, I'd lost two uncles, my paternal grandmother, and my dear Aunty Sherry, who gave me the love I never received from my own mother. At age thirty-one, I lost my beloved father. Too many losses for a young girl, yet somehow those deaths still hadn't left me questioning my mortality.

Another decade passed, and I got married and suffered a near fatal illness, yet when I was at the worst of my illness, I still didn't fear for my life. In fact, I was almost begging to end it. But I lived through it and got my life back.

We've also had to say goodbye to loved ones in Gordon's family. All these deaths have had me wondering how the survivors manage to carry on with their lives while harboring new empty holes in their hearts. How would some manage their finances, and who would care for the ones left behind? I went on an internal tangent about what I would do if I lost my husband. Who would look after me if I got sick? Would I have enough money to live out my old age?

All these new questions had me wondering about my own mortality—the end, when there's no more living. The fears inched up into my subconscious, taking up permanent residence in my worry compartment, ready to stand at attention, receiving a nudge at a moment's notice each time another scary turn of events occurred in my life.

Dying is a part of life, the end result of having had the privilege to live. The life we live is the middle between the two bookends, birth and death, and all the living between the pages becomes the stories people will remember us for. I always felt it morbid to talk about dying, and I'm also superstitious when it comes to speaking out loud about death. I fear I'm opening a door to invite it in as though death were an entity that could hear me speak in the same way that I hope God hears my prayers when I pray. But the fact is that the end of life is inevitable for everyone, whether we think about it or not. No amount of praying, pleading, or wishing to live forever will change that fact.

Sometimes I wonder how people who live well into their nineties must feel after having lived a full life, after having endured the loss of many of their own loved ones and friends by that time. I marvel at how they manage to continue living as they age with the loss of their dear ones. I heard a line in a movie once where an elderly woman sits on a bench in a cemetery after watching her last friend in the world be buried. Another younger woman takes a seat beside her, and the older woman laments, "All my friends have gone now. I'm ready." How awful that must feel, left out in a world with nobody to laugh or cry with, nobody to remember us as we were, who we were, what we've accomplished in life, or what precious memories we hold within while sitting alone day after day, waiting out the end of days. We can only hope that won't be our exit.

No, I certainly don't like to dwell on thoughts about my mortality, but reminders pop up from time to time, which is a normal part of aging once we enter what's called the second half of our lives. It's natural to think about our mortality as life takes its toll around us and we bury our loved ones. Maybe our fears creep in at the midpoint of life more so because age fifty is thought to be the dividing line. In reality, fifty is past midlife, because few people live to one hundred, and the scales already tip closer toward the end of our time on earth than closer to the beginning.

So yes, I'll have my little freak-out moments during which I envision my impending destiny, but I won't allow myself to dwell on it. I'll prepare for the future and live in the now for the time I have left here, grateful for every gifted day I'm still on earth, and I hope that others will remember me in some small way when I'm gone, if only by acknowledging that I once existed.

Inevitability and the Will to Make a Will

We live, we grow, we worry, and although we don't always like to worry or think about the future, it's important to acknowledge it. As one who likes to prepare for tomorrow, I had to agree with Gordon when he suggested we should have wills made to avoid the sticky situations some people fall prey to after losing a loved one and being left to deal with legal repercussions. Living with a senior had prompted me to face such decisions a little sooner than I had expected.

We sometimes assume that nature's course will take the elder spouse first, but there are no guarantees in life, and despite my being younger than Gordon when we married, we decided to do our wills together. Making a will isn't something we like to think about, but making one can help avoid a host of problems in dealing with the difficult time of the loss of a spouse. We took precautions to secure the passing over of our investments, personal effects, and bank accounts. Making a will with a designated beneficiary and executor gave us peace of mind and did not leave the door wide open for the government to get its greedy palms on our estates. We also wanted to sew up our assets to avoid legal and family disputes over who was getting what.

I also discovered legal methods exist to ensure no snags with banks or government interventions occur: This requires designating beneficiaries for investments and home ownership, so Gordon and I made sure we designated one another as beneficiaries with all our investments and insurance policies to ensure the banks wouldn't be able to freeze our accounts until bureaucracy clears if either one of us were to die. We did the same with our many homes by signing joint tenancy to protect us both as sole homeowners and avoid any legal contention or intervention. We've also added provisions for such things as designating who we choose in our living will to take responsibility for decisions on our behalves in case something should happen to either one of us and the other were to be incapacitated.

I once experienced the turmoil of a loved one passing without leaving proper directions in a will, and this caused an unpleasant and somewhat ugly situation that left devastating effects on relationships with other family members. That experience cautioned me enough to know I would never want to cause bad blood for the next generation of inheritors. I learned that tying up loose ends in a neat little bow alleviates those future worries.

This was not one of my favorite chapters to write, but I'll touch on one more important thought here that we should also take into consideration: I think it's important to discuss with our significant others where we'd like our final resting places to be. This is a significant discussion to have, and it's been a thorny one for Gordon and me to come to terms with. Our different religious backgrounds make this discussion an even more delicate situation, because neither of our religions permits us to be buried in the same place.

    I couldn't seem to wrap my head around planning for the inevitable, so I remained perplexed and procrastinating, still apprehensive. I knew that aside from the grief I'd endure if I lost my husband, having to deal with the decision in haste while in a devastated frame of mind would be a difficult feat. Yet I couldn't seem to find comfort in any resolution. I knew in my heart I would want to mourn the loss of my husband in the tradition my religion dictates, and on the same note, I'd also respect his family's wishes and would partake in his own religious protocols. That fateful day would be more painful for me if I refused to cross that bridge and make a decision. I knew if it were me who went first, my husband would have to rely on my sister to look after the plans and place me with other lost loved ones.

    Okay, enough about the grim reaper stuff. I've mentioned it because there are decisions we'll inevitably have to make. Many responsible planners make their reservations ahead of time. I would advise everyone not to be a neglectful avoider like me and plan for that end, because it will eliminate a painful decision to consider while enduring grief. Besides, reserving plots ahead of time can also save money. Supply and demand counts right up until our time of death. If there's no reservation, the charge will be more because of immediate need.

I knew I needed to get my head straight on this matter and take my own advice.

∞ ∞

All that said, admittedly, I sometimes prefer to dodge discussions related to death, even with my husband. I'm one of those people who don't care to bring up unpleasant inevitabilities and talk about funerals, final resting places, or anything pertaining to death. As important as it is for couples to have those discussions, I feel as though I'm tempting the fates by bringing them up. In fact, I've managed to dodge them throughout most of my marriage.

Gordon isn't a man of many words, but his thoughts run deep. When his mind is brewing, I have my secret methods of cajoling him into spitting out what he's thinking. At other times, he may open a conversation out of nowhere. The abstract topic he'll come out with will alert me to a bigger picture, one that informs me what's been whirling around in his brain for some time that has finally pushed its way to the verbal forefront.

One typical morning, waiting for the coffee to brew, I took a seat at the kitchen table after placing Gordon's favorite waffle in the toaster oven. Gordon planted himself in his favorite chair at the table with me and began a conversation that took me by surprise: "I want to be buried with my parents."

My blood ran cold as a sadness overcame me before I spoke. "Where does this come from?" I questioned him with tears in my eyes. "Is this the stuff you're thinking about in your silent, busy mind?" I couldn't shake the discomfort within me as I wondered why after so many years of avoiding discussing the eventual end of one of us, he had chosen that moment to share his wish.

We'd never talked about the subject. We've touched on it, made short references in idle chats, in jest, about what would be our final resting places one day, never ending with any concrete resolution. To Gordon, I'm his world, and he's not comfortable if I'm far away from him. He's often joked about us ending up together in the afterlife, buried together, and I've reminded him several times in those fleeting conversations that because of our different religious backgrounds, being buried together isn't an option. Then we change the subject.

But that morning, Gordon made his wishes clear. It was as though he felt compelled to decide, surrendering his wish of what could never be and moving forward to secure his next best option should something happen to him.

"You know, I just need to know where I'm going next," Gordon said, finalizing his thoughts in true Gordon style. The man who had been a master planner all his life had finally decided where he should go after his time on earth would end with me. It was a final admission to an important decision he'd obviously been giving lots of thought to without consulting me—for the first time in our marriage.

I struggled, wondering how long he'd been hiding his silent thoughts about this decision. I wondered why he was thinking about it now. Was he scared his days were drawing nearer to that inevitable time? I never like to force him to speak. When I notice he's present but a certain glint in his eye signals that his mind is elsewhere, I allow him to process his thoughts, knowing when he's ready to come to terms with a personal dilemma, he'll share it with me. And he did.

My thoughts reverted to the many times we'd joke about silly ideas we had for ourselves to be together in the afterlife, the many times he'd told me he was scared to be without me in eternity. I'd remind him he couldn't come where I was going, and vice versa. He'd then joke about having a TV buried with him, and eventually the conversations would lead to absurdity, because making jokes about our deaths was the only way we both felt comfortable dealing with the subject. The conversations always had the same endings, leaving the unsettled decision to rest.

But the day Gordon came out with his serious decision, it disturbed me and shook me within. I don't know what shook me up most, that he was contemplating his mortality, that he had verbalized his acceptance that we wouldn't be together once we both departed this world, or that he was frightened about his age and health and thought it was time to consider the inevitable.

I couldn't help but wonder whether he had taken it upon himself to make that final decision because he wanted to make sure he had his final say or whether he had been dwelling on the situation and had brought it up because he knew I didn't like to think about death, knowing I would never initiate such a conversation. I didn't ask, because I know my husband is a chronic thinker about tomorrows, sometimes missing the moments of today in his worrying. Despite his silent thoughts, Gordon's issues have a way of floating to the top when he's ready to share, knowing I'm there to listen.

Finality scares me. I never allow myself to imagine my life without Gordon in it, and I didn't want to think about it. I'm not much of a procrastinator, but on the topic of death, I'll force myself to dismiss the thoughts. But Gordon had unwrapped his wishes and placed them in front of me. I opened the box despite my unwillingness to receive. Gordon's resolution forced me to confront my mortality. Although I have spent half my life living independently, the prospect of being left back on my own one day without him scares the crap out of me.

Our life together played out within my thoughts. I don't want to be without Gordon, this man who's been at my side, in my corner, my best friend for twenty years. I'm just unable to conceive of or digest thoughts of what I'll do without him when that inevitable day comes.

Our conversation forced me to think of things I was much more content procrastinating about so I wouldn't have to imagine the inevitable, should Gordon's day come before mine. But he got me thinking enough to consider my own plans. I told Gordon I'd respect his wishes while reaffirming my own wish to be buried near my lost loved ones. Gordon's admission had opened us both up to committing to decide where we'd both go once our ride is over in this life. We heard each other out, drank our coffees, and never mentioned it again until a few months later, after I brought up the conversation with my brother Rory, who happens to be in the same religious predicament with his own marriage.

Feelings of fear and anxiety had me distraught for days after my conversation with Gordon about his wishes. But at an opportune moment with my brother, I felt comfortable in taking the liberty to speak with him about our dilemma. I asked Rory whether he'd considered his final departure or had made any decisions about where he and his wife would be resting. I was pleasantly surprised when he confirmed that he'd done his homework on the matter and had found what he described as a most beautiful cemetery in mid-town where people of any faith could be buried together. I'd never heard of such a place, probably because I'd never had the desire to allow myself to think about the end, let alone initiate such a conversation with my brother.

The next day, I revealed my discovery to Gordon, and he was over the moon with joy. Now, that conversation happened a few months ago, and as of yet, we haven't actually gone to look at those grounds, but Gordon hasn't failed to bring up the subject at least once a week since, eager to lock up our permanent plans to remain together. The decision is made, and that has eliminated the burden of our dilemma. It was a huge relief for us to learn that not even death can separate us.

Epilogue

A good relationship will always be an ongoing work in progress. It shouldn't be laborious or taxing. Rather, marriage should be a continuous effort to keep in mind and practice love, compassion, and understanding. These elements should always be running in the background of our daily activities. When we stop practicing these essential components to keeping a relationship healthy, pieces of us falter and our bonds begin to fray. Relationships need ongoing attention, and we need to make conscious strides to keep them flourishing just as we give TLC to our plants—feeding, nurturing, and caring for them so they'll thrive and continue to bloom.

It's a fact that no matter how much we attempt to avoid waves in our relationships, issues sometimes arise, creating choppy waters to wade through. By choosing to handle our day-to-day lives together in harmony when fate tests the strength of our relationships, we're better able to float those waves together. If we've built that strong foundation from the ground up with love, respect, communication, and compassion, the work shouldn't be difficult even when times present challenges.

We can't sum up a well-lived life by rounding it off to and capping it off at old age. It's the sum of the journey of getting there together and living life to its fullest that sustains and fulfill us to the end destination. When we love with our whole hearts through all that life brings, from celebrations to illness and back to gratitude many times over, navigating through storms and triumphs with unfaltering support and love for one another, we can say we've lived life well. We shouldn't be measuring the quality of our lives by quantities, age limits, or conditions. A good life together envelopes many experiences and emotions, and what matters most is that we remain there for one another despite whatever life may throw our way.

Getting older is a certainty, and falling prey to illness is a gamble we all take when we commit to a relationship—a good bet why "Till death do us part" is a standard part of our wedding vows. Heaven knows Gordon and I both have had our share of illness during our marriage. The fates have tested us many times over, yet we both remain there for one another to support, love, and pick up the slack when the other has no strength to do so. That is love.

Love isn't measured by wealth, status, or how many gifts we receive. We can't ask for love, and love can't be bought or stolen. Love grows from a place in our hearts as each day passes and accumulates in never-ending supply as two people give of themselves and are loyal to one another. When hugs and laughter are plentiful no matter how high the tides roll in to challenge us, love will remain.

Twenty years ago, I questioned myself before committing to marry my husband. I envisioned our life together, tried to predict where we'd be in twenty years, worried about the what-ifs, and took the leap despite my concerns because I knew then that no matter what the universe would throw our way, we'd face it together. I decided not to worry about what I'd do if my older husband got sick or, worse, died and left me behind, because illness takes not only prisoners from the elderly; it chooses its victims at random, at any age.

If we all stepped back in hesitation before committing to marry the people who filled our hearts with love like no other just because we were afraid of what the future might bring, many of us would miss out on fulfilling our hearts.

I realized when I married that I couldn't put a timeline on love or the future. I wanted to envelop the love I'd found for however long God would allow me the privilege. Time became an irrelevant factor, because as long as I knew love would sustain us, it was enough for me.

In moments of uncertain fear,
When my mind wanders obtrusively,
With no leash adhered,
I lie still in my bed,
Taking comfort in knowing you're here.

While the darkness remains,
My fears come to light,
In this time for slumber,
When my worries heed fright.

My lids now draw heavy as consciousness fades,
I rest at peace now relinquishing strife,
Safe in contentment with the melody of your breath,
My best friend, my husband, my partner in life.

End

Thank you for reading *Twenty Years: After "I Do."* If you enjoyed this book, please consider telling your friends and posting a short review by going to my author page on Amazon at:

<u>http://www.amazon.com/author/dgkaye7</u>.

Click on the book cover and then the "Write a review" box.

Word of mouth is an author's best friend and is much appreciated.

About the Author

D.G. Kaye is a Canadian author living in Toronto. She writes nonfiction and memoirs about her life experiences, matters of the heart, and self-help about women's issues. Her positive outlook keeps D.G. on track, allowing her to take on life's challenges with a dose of humor in her quest to overcome adversity.

D.G. began writing when pen and paper became the tools to express her pent-up emotions during her turbulent childhood. She began journaling about her life at a young age and continued writing about the imprints and lessons she learned through people and events she encountered. D.G. writes books to share her stories and inspiration. She advocates for kindness and for women's empowerment. Her favorite saying is "For every kindness received, there should be kindness in return. Wouldn't that just make the world right?"

When she's not writing, D.G. loves to read (self-help books and stories of triumph), cook (concocting new recipes, never to come out the same way twice), shop (only if it's a great sale), play poker (when she gets the chance), and, most of all, travel.

Disclaimer

Twenty Years: After "I Do" is a work of nonfiction. This book was written according to the author's recollection of events in her own life. The author has changed and omitted some names in order to maintain the anonymity of those mentioned. Any medical and financial references in this book are written solely from the author's experience, and she advises her readers to always seek medical and financial advice to suit their own individual needs.

Acknowledgments

Thank you to my sister-in-law Katy and my friend Doris for reading this book in its early stages, and thank you to my many author friends who have offered their feedback the many times I requested it. You know who you are.

As always, I'd like to thank my editor, Talia Leduc of Northwest Editing, and my book cover artist, Yvonne Less of Art 4 Artists. I'd also like to thank David Cronin at Moyhill Publishing for his wonderful formatting and typesetting services.

Visit D.G.'s author pages:

www.amazon.com/author/dgkaye7

www.goodreads.com/dgkaye

Contact D.G. at:

author@dgkayewriter.com

Follow D.G. on her social sites:

www.twitter.com/@pokercubster

www.facebook.com/dgkaye

www.linkedin.com/in/dgkaye7

www.google.com/+DebbyDGKayeGies

www.pinterest.com/dgkaye7

www.instagram.com/dgkaye

www.stumbleupon.com/stumbler/DGKaye

Other Books by D.G. Kaye

P.S. I Forgive You
A Broken Legacy

Purchase link:
www.smarturl.it/bookPSIForgiveYou

"I hurt for her. She wasn't much of a mother, but she was still my mother."

Confronted with resurfacing feelings of guilt, D.G. Kaye is tormented by her decision to remain estranged from her dying emotionally abusive mother after resolving to banish her years ago, an event she has shared in her book *Conflicted Hearts*. In *P.S. I Forgive You*, Kaye takes us on a compelling heartfelt journey as she seeks to understand the roots of her mother's narcissism, let go of past hurts, and find forgiveness for both her mother and herself.

After struggling for decades to break free, Kaye has severed the unhealthy ties that bound her to her dominating mother—but now Kaye battles new confliction, as the guilt she harbors over her decision only increases as the end of her mother's life draws near. Kaye once again struggles with her conscience and her feelings of being obligated to return to a painful past she thought she left behind.

Excerpt — Aftermath

My mother is dead.

She had been dying for so many years that when the day finally came, my heart was drowning in a swirling abyss of guilt. The years of emotional turmoil I had pent up as the daughter of a narcissistic mother had reached their denouement.

My anger and past resentment toward my mother had turned into an inquisition, a searching of my soul. I needed to understand the root of her ego. It was not enough for me to lay her body to rest. I needed to fill in the gaps, find out what had spurred the injustices she inflicted on so many, and clear the debris lingering in my own conscience to make peace with my past and send her off with my forgiveness.

I had realized how emotionally toxic it was to hang on to hurt and resentment, but the death of my emotionally abusive mother didn't necessarily end the residual hurt of being abused. To set my heart free, I needed to seek out a path to resolve past hurts and the conflict that had tainted my memories.

I'll never know if peace waits for my mother on the other side. I wonder if the afterlife offers second chances to wrongdoers or if they learn lessons from the injustices they commit while on earth. I'd like to think God has mercy and has welcomed my mother into heaven with the same forgiveness I have granted her after learning to surrender my resentments. Looking back, I have realized what a lost soul my mother really was.

Through all her theatrics, lies, and betrayals as she portrayed herself as the person she wanted to be, or perhaps believed she was, my mother harbored a damaged soul that didn't know how to dig itself out. The same persona she had created to shine in the limelight, to acquire anything she desired, or to disguise her insecurities ironically became her downfall.

This story is the aftermath, my way of coming to terms with and relinquishing the guilt and instilled fears I have carried from childhood. It is my decision to banish my mother from my life and a resolution to find peace within myself with my decision.

Conflicted Hearts
A Daughter's Quest for Solace from Emotional Guilt

Purchase link:
www.smarturl.it/bookconflictedhearts

"Somehow I believed it was my obligation to try to do the right thing by her because she had given birth to me."

Burdened with constant worry for her father and the guilt caused by her mother's narcissism, D.G. Kaye had a short childhood. When she moved away from home at eighteen, she began to grow into herself, overcoming her lack of guidance and her insecurities.

Her life experiences became her teachers, and she learned from the mistakes and choices she made along the way, plagued by the guilt she carried for her mother.

Conflicted Hearts is a heartfelt journey of self-discovery and acceptance, an exploration of the quest for solace from emotional guilt.

Words We Carry
Essays of Obsession and Self-Esteem

Purchase link:
www.smarturl.it/bookwordswecarry

"I have been a great critic of myself for most of my life, and I was darned good at it, deflating my own ego without the help of anyone else."

What do our shopping habits, high-heeled shoes, and big hair have to do with how we perceive ourselves? Do the slights we endured when we were young affect how we choose our relationships now? D.G. takes us on a journey, unlocking the hurts of the past by identifying situations that hindered her own self-esteem. Her anecdotes and confessions demonstrate how the hurtful events in our lives linger and set the tone for how we value our own self-worth. *Words We Carry* is a raw, personal accounting of how the author overcame the demons of low self-esteem with the determination to learn to love herself.

MenoWhat? A Memoir
Memorable Moments of Menopause

Purchase link:
www.smarturl.it/bookMenoWhatAMemoir

"I often found myself drifting from a state of normal in a sudden twist of bitchiness."

From PMS to menopause to what the hell?

D.G. adds a touch of humor to a tale about a not-so-humorous time. While bidding farewell to her dearly departing estrogen, D.G. struggles to tame her raging hormones of fire, relentless dryness, flooding and droughts and other unflattering symptoms.

Join D.G. on her meno-journey to slay the dragons of menopause as she tries to hold on to her sanity, memory, hair, and so much more!

Have Bags, Will Travel
Trips and Tales: Memoirs of an Over-packer

Purchase link:
www.smarturl.it/bookHaveBags

D.G. Kaye is back, and as she reflects on some of her more memorable vacations and travel snags, she finds herself constantly struggling to keep one step ahead of the ever-changing guidelines of the airlines—with her overweight luggage in tow. Her stories alert us to some of the pitfalls of being an obsessive shopper, especially when it comes time for D.G. to bring her treasures home, and remind us of the simpler days when traveling was a breeze.

In her quest to keep from tipping the scales, D.G. strives to devise new tricks to fit everything in her suitcases on each trip. Why is she consistently a target for Canada customs on her return journeys?

D.G.'s witty tales take us from airports, to travel escapades with best friends, to reflections on how time can change the places we hold dear in our hearts. Her memories will entertain and have you reminiscing about some of your own most treasured journeys—and perhaps make you contemplate revamping your packing strategies.

www.ingramcontent.com/pod-product-compliance
Lightning Source LLC
LaVergne TN
LVHW041256080426
835510LV00009B/756